# The
# U.K. to U.S.A.
# DICTIONARY

by Claudine Dervaes and John Hunter

ISBN 0-933143-49-4
   Library of Congress Control Number: 2005900441

*Solitaire Publishing, Inc.*
*1090 S. Chateau Pt.*
*Inverness, FL 34450-3565*
*(352) 726-5026*
*e-mail: PSolitaire@aol.com*

*THANK YOU FOR HAVING PURCHASED*

# The
# U.K. to U.S.A.
# Dictionary

We welcome your comments and suggestions.

This book is available through many specialty British shops in the U.S. or may be special ordered by bookstores.

If you would like to order another copy, send your name and address (U.S. addresses only) along with a check or money order for $7.50 to

*Solitaire Publishing, Inc.*
*1090 S. Chateau Pt.*
*Inverness, FL 34450-3565*
*(352) 726-5026*
*e-mail: PSolitaire@aol.com*

# TABLE OF CONTENTS

# PREFACE

Meanings of some of the words in this dictionary may be obvious. Others can cause confusion/misunderstanding when used in the U.S. or in the U.K.

Some slang words are included but their listing does not condone the use of any derogatory/negative expression. Words generally used throughout Britain and the U.S. have been chosen as opposed to ones that may be used in a certain region or locale. The Welsh language has not been included – it is completely distinct.

IT IS ALSO IMPORTANT TO NOTE THAT SPELLINGS WILL DIFFER, such as the British vs. American spellings for centre/center, theatre/theater, civilised/civilized, manoeuver/maneuver, realise/realize, computerise/computerize. Pronunciation will also vary and we have provided a brief list of some of the words that are pronounced differently. We welcome your comments and suggestions.

ABBREVIATIONS USED:

| | |
|---|---|
| abbr. | abbreviation |
| colloq. | colloquial |
| dial. | dialect |
| n. | noun |
| N.Eng. | Northern England |
| punc. | punctuation |
| Sc. | Scottish |
| v. | verb |

Thank you.

# U.K.
# to
# U.S.A.

**BRITISH WORDS/EXPRESSIONS
AND U.S. COUNTERPARTS**

| U.K. | U.S.A. |
|------|--------|

## A

| | |
|------|--------|
| **A BIT OFF** | somewhat annoying, unfair |
| **ACCLIMATISED** | acclimated |
| **ACID DROP** | hard candy with a bitter taste |
| **ADVERT** | advertisement/commercial |
| **AERIAL** | antenna |
| **AERODROME/PLANE** | airdrome/plane |
| **AFTERS** | dessert |
| **AGLEY** (dialect) | off the intended route/awry |
| **"A" LEVELS** | "advanced" high school exams |
| **ANKLE-BITER** | rug rat |
| **ANORAK** | parka |
| **ANTI-CLOCKWISE** | counter-clockwise |
| **APPROVED SCHOOL** | juvenile detention center |
| **ARSE** | ass, buttocks |
| **ARTICULATED LORRY** | tractor trailer |
| **AS HAPPY AS A SAND BOY** | as happy as a lark |
| **AT A PINCH** | in a pinch |
| **AUBERGINE** | eggplant |
| **AULD LANG SYNE** | the old days |
| **AUTUMN** | fall |

## B

| | |
|------|--------|
| **BACCY** | tobacco |

| U.K. | U.S.A. |
|---|---|
| **BACK BENCHER** | Member of Parliament not a Minister |
| **BACKHANDERS** | kickbacks |
| **BACK OF BEYOND** | the sticks, the boonies |
| **BAD FORM** | bad manners, poor behavior |
| **BADMASH** | ruffian |
| **BAFFIES** (Sc.) | slippers |
| **BAGS** | many, lots |
| **BAKER-LEGGED** | knock-kneed |
| **BAKING TRAY** | cookie sheet |
| **BALLS/BALLS-UP** | foul-up, messed up |
| **BANGER** | sausage |
| **BANGER** | firecracker |
| **BANGERS AND MASH** | sausages and mashed potatoes |
| **BANG ON** | just right, terrific |
| **BANK HOLIDAY** | legal holiday |
| **BANK NOTE** | bill |
| **BANNED** (from driving) | license suspended |
| **BANNOCK** (Sc.) | unleavened oatmeal cake |
| **BAP** | hamburger bun |
| **BARGEE** | person working on a barge |
| **BARM CAKE** | hamburger bun |
| **BARMY** | crazy/silly |
| **BARRISTER** | lawyer able to appear in the upper courts |
| **BARTON** | farm yard |
| **BASH** | try, attempt |

| U.K. | U.S.A. |
|---|---|
| BATMAN | British Army Officer's Orderly |
| BATHERS | bathing suit |
| BAWBEE (dialect) | trifle/insignificant thing |
| BEADLE | church official |
| BEAK | school headmaster/justice of the peace |
| BEANO/BEANFEAST | employer's annual dinner/ any celebration dinner |
| BEASTLY | very unpleasant |
| BED ONLY | hotel room without meals |
| BEDROOM ENSUITE | room with a private bath |
| BEDSIDE LOCKER | nightstand |
| BEDSIT/TER | one room apt. sometimes including kitchen; studio |
| BEER & SKITTLES | pleasure, amusement |
| BEETLE CRUSHERS | heavy boots |
| BELISHA BEACON | flashing amber light at a pedestrian crossing |
| BEN (Sc.) | a mountain peak |
| BERK/BURK | jerk |
| BESPOKE or MADE TO MEASURE | custom-made |
| BETTING SHOP | licensed public betting office |
| BIFFIN | red cooking apple |
| BIG DIPPER | roller-coaster |
| BILL (restaurant) | check or tab |
| BILL (account) | account |

3

| U.K. | U.S.A. |
|---|---|
| **BILL'S MOTHER'S** | a catchphrase, e.g. "looks dark over Bill's Mother's" |
| **BILLYCOCK** (N.Eng.) | derby hat |
| **BIN LINER** | trash bag |
| **BIRO** | ballpoint pen |
| **BIRTHDAY HONOR'S LIST** | list of people who have titles given to them on the sovereign's birthday |
| **BISCUIT** (sweet) | cookie |
| **BISCUIT** | cracker |
| **BIT OF A LAD** | a ladies' man |
| **BLACK OR WHITE** (coffee) | without or with cream |
| **BLACKLEG/SCAB** | scab (strike breaker) |
| **BLACK MARIA** | police van |
| **BLACK TREACLE** | molasses |
| **BLANCMANGE** | vanilla pudding |
| **BLIGHTER** | mean person |
| **BLIMEY** (slang) | an oath (from "blind me") |
| **BLIND** (window) | shade |
| **BLINDER (TO PLAY A)** | to do really well |
| **BLOCK OF FLATS** | apartment house/building |
| **BLOKE** | man or fellow |
| **BLOODY** (slang) | expletive, used with other words to mean huge. For example, a "bloody big house," also means very, such as "bloody well" |

4

| U.K. | U.S.A. |
|---|---|
| **BLOODY-MINDED** | obstinate |
| **BLOOMER** | mistake or blooper |
| **BLOOMING** (slang) | used like the word bloody |
| **BLOW THE GAFF** | give away a secret/plot |
| **BLUE-EYED BOY** | fair-haired boy, favorite |
| **BLUE FUNK** | state of fright/terror |
| **BOARD** | interview, review, or promotion panel |
| **BOB'S YOUR UNCLE** | all is well |
| **BOBBY** | police officer |
| **BOBBY-DAZZLER** | remarkable, notable |
| **BOILED SWEET** | hard candy |
| **BOLLARD** | traffic cone, barricade |
| **BOLLOCKS** (slang) | testicles, nuts, rocks |
| **BONCE** | person's head |
| **BONKERS** | crazy |
| **BONNET** (auto) | hood |
| **BONNY** | pretty, attractive |
| **BOOK** | make reservations |
| **BOOK-IN** | check-in |
| **BOOK POST** | postage for mailing books |
| **BOOK TOKEN** | gift certificate redeemable for books |
| **BOOT** (auto) | trunk |
| **BORSTAL** | juvenile detention center |
| **BOSH** | nonsense |
| **BOTHER** | expresses impatience |

| U.K. | U.S.A. |
|---|---|
| **BOTHY** (Sc.) | cottage, hut |
| **BOTTOM DRAWER** | hope chest |
| **BOTTOM GEAR** | first gear/lowest gear |
| **BOUGHT A PUP** | deceived, swindled |
| **BOWLER** | derby hat |
| **BOWLS** | lawn bowling |
| **BOXING DAY** | December 26 |
| **BOX ROOM** | storeroom (house) |
| **BOX SPANNER** | socket wrench |
| **BRACES** | suspenders |
| **BRACKETS** (punc.) | parentheses |
| **BRAE** (Sc.) | hillside |
| **BRASS FARTHING** | a tiny amount of money, a plugged nickel |
| **BRAW** (Sc.) | good, fine |
| **BREAD AND BUTTER PUDDING** | bread pudding |
| **BREAK** | recess at school, work etc. |
| **BREAKER'S YARD** | scrap iron dealer, junkyard |
| **BREEZE BLOCK** | cinder/cement block |
| **BRIDGE ROLL** | hot dog bun |
| **BRIEF** | attorney engaged by a client |
| **BRING AND BUY SALE** | swap meet |
| **BROAD BEAN** | lima bean |
| **BROLLY** | umbrella |
| **BROTHEL KREEPERS** | soft-soled shoes |
| **BROWNED OFF** | fed up, bored |

6

| U.K. | U.S.A. |
|---|---|
| **BROWN STUDY (IN A)** | daydreaming |
| **BUBBLE & SQUEAK** | cold meat fried with cabbage and potatoes |
| **BUCKSHEE** | something free/a gift |
| **BUGGER** (slang) | term of abuse or affection; annoying person, or when affectionately a scamp or a rascal |
| **BUGGER ALL** (slang) | nothing |
| **BUGGER OFF** (slang) | get out of my face, get lost |
| **BUILDING SOCIETY** | organization providing loans (especially for house purchases) and investment accounts |
| **BULLRUSH** | cattail |
| **BULLY BEEF** | corned beef |
| **BUMF** | paperwork/toilet paper |
| **BUMPERSHOOT** | term for umbrella, not used anymore |
| **BUNCHES** (hair) | pigtails |
| **BUNFIGHT** | tea party |
| **BUNGED UP** | stopped up |
| **BUNS** | muffins/cupcakes |
| **BURGLE** | burglarize |
| **BURN** (Sc.) | small stream or brook |
| **BUSBY/BEARSKIN** | guardsman's tall fur hat |

| U.K. | U.S.A. |
|------|--------|
| **BUSKING** | entertaining on the streets for money |
| **BUT AND BEN** (Sc.) | two-roomed cottage |
| **BUTTONHOLE** | boutonniere |
| **BUTTONS** | bellboy |
| **BUTTY, BUTTIES** | sandwich, sandwiches |
| **BYRE** | cowshed |

# C

| U.K. | U.S.A. |
|------|--------|
| **C.V. (Curriculum Vitae)** | resume |
| **CABOOSE** | ship's galley |
| **CACK-HANDED** | clumsy, awkward |
| **CAFÉ** | sometimes pronounced "caff" |
| **CAKES AND ALE** | the good things of life |
| **CAKE-HOLE** (slang) | mouth |
| **CALL BOX** | phone booth |
| **CALLOVER** (betting) | announcing the latest odds |
| **CANDY FLOSS** | cotton candy |
| **CANNON** (billiards) | carom |
| **CANTEEN OF CUTLERY** | boxed set of cutlery |
| **CAP** (sports) | special hat awarded to members of International sports teams |

| U.K. | U.S.A. |
|---|---|
| **CAPSTAN LATHE** | turret lathe |
| **CARAVAN** | trailer (recreational) |
| **CARAVANETTE** | small R.V. (recreational vehicle) |
| **CAR BOOT SALE** | temporary flea market where goods are displayed on car trunks |
| **CAR HIRE** | car rental |
| **CAREER** (vehicle out of control) | careen |
| **CARETAKER/PORTER** | janitor |
| **CAR PARK** | parking lot |
| **CARRIAGE PAID** | free shipping |
| **CARRIAGEWAY** | highway |
| **CARRY ON** | continue |
| **CASTER SUGAR** | white, finely granulated sugar |
| **CASUALTY** | emergency room |
| **CATAPULT** | slingshot |
| **CATHERINE WHEEL** | pinwheel firework |
| **CAT-MINT** | catnip |
| **CAT'S EYES** | reflectors on roads |
| **CATTLE GRID** | Texas gate, cattle guard |
| **CENTRAL RESERVATION** | median |
| **CHALK AND CHEESE** | meaning "as different as" such as night and day |
| **CHAR** (cup of) | tea |

9

| U.K. | U.S.A. |
|---|---|
| CHARABANC | tour bus/motorcoach |
| CHARLADY | housemaid/cleaning maid |
| CHARTERED ACCOUNTANT | certified public accountant |
| CHASE | unenclosed tract of land |
| CHEAP AND NASTY | low cost and poor quality |
| CHEEK | nerve |
| CHEEKY | sassy |
| CHEERIO | goodbye |
| CHEESED OFF | bored, exasperated |
| CHEMIST | pharmacist |
| CHEMIST SHOP | pharmacy/drugstore |
| CHEST OF DRAWERS | dresser |
| CHILD-MINDER | babysitter |
| CHINWAG | talk, chatter |
| CHIP BOARD | particle board |
| CHIPPY | fish and chips shop |
| CHIPS | french fries |
| CHIROPODIST | podiatrist |
| CHIT | voucher, receipt |
| CHIVVY | to chase/to hurry up |
| CHOCK A BLOCK | jammed or crowded |
| CHORLEY CAKE | small round pastry filled with sultanas (golden raisins) |
| CHUFFED | pleased |
| CIDER | alcoholic cider/hard cider |
| CINEMA | movie house/theater |

| U.K. | U.S.A. |
|---|---|
| **CITY CENTRE** | downtown |
| **CITY EDITOR** | newspaper editor of business/finance |
| **CLANGER** | blunder |
| **CLASS/FORM** | (school) grade |
| **CLEARWAY** | road where stopping is prohibited |
| **CLERK OF WORKS** | construction overseer |
| **CLEVER DICK** | know-it-all, smart-alec |
| **CLIPPIE** | old term for woman who collects fares on buses, etc. |
| **CLOAKROOM** | checkroom |
| **CLOAKROOM ATTENDANT** | hat/coat check person |
| **CLOBBER** | clothing |
| **CLOCK** (slang) | hit |
| **CLOTH CAP** | blue collar worker |
| **CLOTHES PEG** | clothes pin |
| **CLOTTED CREAM** | milk thickened by scalding |
| **CLOUGH** | narrow valley |
| **COACH** | bus |
| **COARSE FISH/FISHING** | fresh water fish/fishing, excluding salmon and trout |
| **COB** | round crisp loaf of bread |
| **COBBLERS** | nonsense, bunk |
| **COCK-A-HOOP** | elated |
| **COCK A SNOOK** | to thumb one's nose |
| **COCK-UP** | mistake or blooper |

| U.K. | U.S.A. |
|---|---|
| **CODLING** | a cooking apple |
| **CODSWALLOP** | gibberish/nonsense |
| **COCKEREL** | rooster |
| **COLD COMFORT** | little consolation. From Stella Gibbons' book <u>Cold Comfort Farm</u> |
| **COLLAR STIFFENER AND STUD** | collar stay and button |
| **COLLECT** | pick up or call for |
| **COLLIERY** | coal mine with buildings |
| **COMBS** (abbreviation for combinations) | combined underwear, long johns |
| **COMMERCIAL TRAVELER** | traveling sales rep |
| **COMMISSIONAIRE** | uniformed door person at theaters, etc. |
| **COMMUNICATION CORD** | emergency handle |
| **COMPERE** | show host/master of ceremonies |
| **CONJURER** | magician |
| **CONKERS** | game played with horse chestnuts on strings |
| **CONSCRIPT** | draftee |
| **CONSCRIPTION** | the draft |
| **CONSTABLE** | police officer |
| **CONSTABULARY** | police force |
| **COOKER** | stove/range |
| **COOKERY BOOK** | cookbook |

| U.K. | U.S.A. |
|---|---|
| **COOK THE BOOKS** | falsify records |
| **COPPER** (slang) | policeman |
| **COPSE** | small wooded area |
| **CORACLE** | small wickerwork boat |
| **CORN FLOUR** | cornstarch |
| **CORNISH PASTY** | meat and vegetable turnover |
| **CORPORATION** | city government |
| **COSH** | blackjack/bludgeon |
| **COS LETTUCE** | romaine lettuce |
| **COSTERMONGER** | street seller of fruits, fish, etc. |
| **COT** | baby bed/crib |
| **COTTAGE LOAF** | loaf of bread made from two pieces, a smaller one on top of a larger one |
| **COTTON REEL** | thread spool |
| **COTTON WOOL** | cotton balls/cotton pads/ absorbent cotton |
| **COURGETTE** | zucchini |
| **COURIER** | tour escort, tour conductor |
| **COURT SHOES** | pumps |
| **COW PAT** | cow chip (dung) |
| **COWSLIP** | marsh marigold |
| **CRANE FLY** | daddy-long-legs, harvestman |
| **CREAM CRACKER** | soda cracker |
| **CRECHE/NURSERY** | day care facility |

13

| U.K. | U.S.A. |
|---|---|
| CRISPS | chips (potato) |
| CROWD PULLER | drawing card/draw |
| CRUMPET | English muffin |
| CRY OFF | beg off |
| CRYSTALLISED FRUIT | candied fruit |
| CUDDY (Sc.) | donkey |
| CULPABLE HOMICIDE (Sc.) | manslaughter |
| CULVER | pigeon/dove |
| CUPBOARD | closet |
| CUPPA | cup of tea |
| CUPS (IN ONE'S) | while drunk |
| CURD CHEESE | cottage cheese |
| CURRENT ACCOUNT | checking account |
| CUTE | ingenious, clever, attractive |
| CUT THROAT RAZOR | straight razor |
| CUTLERY | silverware, flatware |

# D

| | |
|---|---|
| DAFT | silly, foolish |
| DARBIES | handcuffs |
| DARBY AND JOAN CLUB | club for the elderly |
| DAVENPORT | writing desk, bureau |
| DAY TRIPPERS | people on one-day outings |

| U.K. | U.S.A. |
|---|---|
| **DEAR** | expensive |
| **DEASIL** (Sc.) | clockwise |
| **DEATH DUTY** | inheritance tax |
| **DECOKE** (auto) | head/valve job |
| **DEKKO** | look |
| **DEMERARA SUGAR** | raw brown sugar |
| **DEMOB.** | military discharge |
| **DEPOSIT ACCOUNT** | savings account |
| **DESICCATED** (coconut) | shredded |
| **DIAMANTE** | rhinestone |
| **DICEY/DODGY** | problematic/risky |
| **DICKEY SEAT** | rumble seat |
| **DIDDLE** | swindle, cheat |
| **DIGS** | lodgings |
| **DINNER HOUR** | lunch break |
| **DINNER LADY** (school) | cafeteria lady |
| **DIP** | switch vehicle's lights to low beam |
| **DIRECTORY ENQUIRIES** | information |
| **DISORIENTATED** | disoriented |
| **DISTRICT** | precinct |
| **DIVER** (bird) | loon |
| **DIVERSION** | detour |
| **DOCH AND DORRIS (WEE)** (Sc.) | drink before leaving, one for the road |
| **DOCKET** | label listing contents |

| | |
|---|---|
| **DOING A BOMB** | successful |
| **DOLE (THE)** | unemployment benefit from the state |
| **DONKEY'S YEARS** | dog's age |
| **DOSS, DOSS DOWN** | lie down |
| **DOSS HOUSE** | cheap lodging, flop house |
| **DOUBLE** (billiards) | bank shot |
| **DOWNS** | hills |
| **DRAPERS** | fabric store |
| **DRAUGHT EXCLUDER** | weather stripping |
| **DRAUGHTS** | checkers |
| **DRAWING PIN** | thumbtack |
| **DRESS CIRCLE** | mezzanine/loge |
| **DRESSING GOWN** | bathrobe |
| **DROP A BRICK** | be indiscreet |
| **DROP A CLANGER** | make a big mistake |
| **DUCK EGG** (cricket) | out without scoring, goose egg |
| **DUAL CARRIAGEWAY** | divided highway |
| **DUFF** | boiled/steamed flour pudding |
| **DUFF GEN** | bum steer |
| **DUFF SPARES** | bad parts |
| **DUMMY** (child's) | pacifier |
| **DUSTBIN** | trash can |
| **DUSTCART** | garbage truck |
| **DUSTMAN** | sanitary engineer |

| U.K. | U.S.A. |
|---|---|
| **DUSTY (NOT SO)** | fairly good |
| **DUTCH CAP** | birth control diaphragm |

# E

| U.K. | U.S.A. |
|---|---|
| **EACH WAY BET** | win or place |
| **EARTH/EARTHWIRE** (electrical) | ground/groundwire |
| **ECCLES CAKE** | round pastry cake filled with currants |
| **EGGS AND SOLDIERS** | boiled eggs and toast strips |
| **EIDERDOWN** | comforter |
| **ELASTOPLAST** | band-aid |
| **ELEVENSES** | morning coffee break |
| **ELDRITCH** (Sc.) | weird, hideous |
| **EMULSION PAINT** | flat paint |
| **END OF YOUR TETHER** | end of your rope |
| **ENGAGED** (phone) | busy |
| **ENGLISH BREAKFAST** | cereal, eggs, sausages, bacon, tomatoes, tea, mushrooms, fried bread |
| **ENTREE** | meal before the main course |
| **ESQ./ESQUIRE** (example: J.Smith, Esq.) | title for a man when Mr. is not used |

| U.K. | U.S.A. |
|---|---|
| **ESTATE AGENT** | realtor |
| **ESTATE CAR** | station wagon |
| **SHOOTING BRAKE** | |
| **EX-DIRECTORY** | unlisted number |
| **EXTENSION LEAD** | extension cord |

# F

| U.K. | U.S.A. |
|---|---|
| **FACE FLANNEL** | washcloth |
| **FAG** | cigarette |
| **FAGGOT** | seasoned chopped liver roll |
| **FANCY/FANCIED** | want or like, wanted or liked |
| **FANNY** | vagina |
| **FASH** (Sc.) | trouble, bother |
| **FATHER CHRISTMAS** | Santa Claus |
| **FED UP** | annoyed, frustrated |
| **FEEDER** | child's bib/bottle |
| **FELL** | mountain, hill, high moorland |
| **FILLING STATION** | gas station |
| **FILM** | movie |
| **FIRE BRIGADE** | fire department |
| **FIRST FLOOR** | second floor |
| **FISH MONGER** | dealer in fish |
| **FISH SLICE** | spatula |

| U.K. | U.S.A. |
|---|---|
| **FITTED CARPET** | wall-to-wall carpet |
| **FIVER** | five pound note |
| **FIVES** | handball |
| **FIXTURES** (sports) | schedule |
| **FLAG DAY** | tag day |
| **FLAT** | apartment |
| **FLAUTIST** | flutist |
| **FLEX** | electric cord |
| **FLICK KNIFE** | switchblade |
| **FLIT** (Sc.) | move house |
| **FLUID OUNCE** (U.K.) | 0.9606 U.S. fluid ounces |
| **FLUTTER** | small bet |
| **FLY** | alert, astute |
| **FLYOVER** | overpass |
| **FOOTBALL** | soccer |
| **FORCE** | small waterfall |
| **FORTNIGHT** | two weeks |
| **FRANKING MACHINE** | postage meter |
| **FREE HOUSE, FREE OFF LICENCE** | pub, liquor store not tied to a brewery |
| **FRIGATE** (ship) | small destroyer |
| **FRILLY** | lacy |
| **FRINGE** (hair) | bangs |
| **FROWSTY** | musty, stale smelling |
| **FRUIT MACHINE** | slot machine |
| **FUBSY** | fat, squat |

| U.K. | U.S.A. |
|------|--------|
| **FULL MARKS** | highest grade |
| **FULL MONTY** | the whole thing |
| **FULL STOP** (punc.) | period |
| **FUNNY BONE** | crazy bone |

# G

| U.K. | U.S.A. |
|------|--------|
| **GAFFER** | foreman, old man |
| **GALLERY** | balcony |
| **GALLON** (U.K.) | 1.2 U.S. gallons |
| **GAMMON** | ham steak |
| **GAMMY** (leg) | slighty lame |
| **GAMP** | large umbrella |
| **GAMS** | legs (usually female) |
| **GANGWAY** | aisle |
| **GAOL/GAOLER** | jail/jailer |
| **GARDEN** | yard |
| **GARTH** | paddock, close |
| **GASH** | spare, extra |
| **GATEAU** | layered cake |
| **GAZUMP** | raise the agreed price of a house after receiving a better offer |
| **GEAR LEVER** | gear stick |
| **GEN** | information |

| U.K. | U.S.A. |
|---|---|
| **GET CRACKING** | get going |
| **GET KNOTTED** | stop annoying me |
| **GET STUCK INTO** | eat, enjoy |
| **GET STUFFED** | get lost |
| **GET THE HUMP** | become irritated, sulk |
| **GET THE PUSH** | to be fired, sacked |
| **GEYSER** (gas) | water heater |
| **GHOULIES/GOOLIES** | testicles |
| **GILL, GHYLL** | mountain torrent, ravine |
| **GINGER NUT** | ginger snap |
| **GIRL GUIDE** | girl scout |
| **GIVE OVER** | give up |
| **GIVE WAY** | yield |
| **GLEN** (Sc.) | narrow valley |
| **GLOVE BOX** | glove compartment |
| **GOBBET** | small amount |
| **GOB** (slang) | mouth |
| **GOB STOPPER** | jaw breaker |
| **GO FOR A BURTON** | lost, destroyed, killed |
| **GOODS/GOODS WAGON** | freight/freight truck |
| **GOODS LIFT** | freight elevator |
| **GOOGLY** | curve ball |
| **GOOLIES** (slang) | testicles, nuts, rocks |
| **GORBLIMEY/BLIMEY** | expression of surprise or indignation |
| **GORMLESS** | stupid, lacking sense |
| **GO SLOW** | worker's slow down |

21

| U.K. | U.S.A. |
|---|---|
| GO SPARE | become very annoyed |
| GRADELY | excellent, handsome |
| GRAMMAR SCHOOL | high school |
| GREAT COAT | military overcoat |
| GREASEPROOF PAPER | waxed paper |
| GREENFLY | green aphid, plant louse |
| GREENGROCER | retailer of fruit and vegetables |
| GREEN PEPPER | bell pepper |
| GREET (Sc.) | weep, cry |
| GRIFF | news, reliable information |
| GRILL | broil |
| GRIZZLE | whine, sob |
| GROUND FLOOR | first floor |
| GROUNDAGE | port taxes |
| GUARD (train) | conductor |
| GUARD'S VAN (train) | caboose |
| GUBBINS | gadgets, useless items |
| GUDGEON PIN | wrist pin |
| GUM | glue or paste |
| GUY (FAWKES) | effigy of Guy Fawkes burnt on November 5 |
| GYMKHANA | competition for horse riding and jumping |
| GYP (GIVE SOMEONE) | torment, treat unmercifully |

# H

| U.K. | U.S.A. |
|------|--------|
| **HABERDASHERY** | notions store |
| **HAIR CLIP** | barrette |
| **HAIR GRIP** | bobby pin |
| **HAIR SLIDE** | barette |
| **HALF-ROUNDS** | sandwiches made from half slices of bread |
| **HALF-TERM** (holiday) | semester/term break |
| **HALT** | a way station, whistle-stop |
| **HANDBAG** | purse |
| **HAND OFF** (rugby) | push away opponent with palm of hand |
| **HANGER** | wooded area on a steep, sloping hill |
| **HA'P'ORTH** (half-penny worth) | slightest, minute quantity |
| **HARD BAKED/BOILED** | cynical, disillusioned |
| **HARDCORE** | broken bricks and rocks used for road foundations |
| **HARD LINES** | bad luck |
| **HARD SHOULDER** | emergency lane |
| **HARL** (Sc.) | drag along the ground |
| **HAVE A GO** | give it a try |
| **HAVER** | talk foolishly/babble, hesitate |
| **HEADMASTER/MISTRESS** | principal |

| U.K. | U.S.A. |
|---|---|
| **HEATH** | open land, covered with low shrubs, usually heather |
| **HEATH ROBINSON** | absurdly ingenious and impractical |
| **HELTER-SKELTER** | corkscrew slide |
| **HIDE** | blind (hunting or observing) |
| **HIGH TEA** | evening meal |
| **HIRE CAR** | rental car |
| **HIRE PURCHASE** | installment plan |
| **HOARDING** | billboard, signboard |
| **HOB** | stove top |
| **HOBNAIL BOOTS** | jackboots |
| **HOCKEY** | field hockey |
| **HOCUS-POCUS** | jiggery-pokery |
| **HOGMANAY** (Sc.) | New Year's Eve Celebration |
| **HOLIDAY** | vacation |
| **HOLME** | land around river that is subject to flooding |
| **HOMELY** (person) | pleasant and unpretentious |
| **HOOTER** | horn, siren |
| **HOOTER** | nose |
| **HOUSING ESTATE** | subdivision |
| **HUM** | unpleasant smell |
| **HUMBUG** | minty, hard-boiled candy |
| **HUNDREDWEIGHT** | 112 pounds |
| **HUNDREDS AND THOUSANDS** | nonpareil |

| U.K. | U.S.A. |
|---|---|

# I

| | |
|---|---|
| **ICE CREAM CORNET** | ice cream cone |
| **ICED LOLLY** | popsicle |
| **ICING SUGAR** | powdered/confectioner's sugar |
| **IDENTIFICATION PARADE** | line up |
| **IMMERSION HEATER** | electric water heater |
| **INCH** | small Scottish island |
| **INFANT SCHOOL** | school for those age 5-7 |
| **INGLE** | fire burning in hearth |
| **INGLE NOOK** | corner by a fireplace |
| **INJECTION** | shot |
| **INLAND REVENUE** | internal revenue |
| **INSECT** | bug |
| **INTAKE** | batch of recruits |
| **INTERIOR SPRUNG** | innerspring |
| **INTERVAL** | intermission |
| **INVERTED COMMAS** | quotation marks |
| **INVIGILATOR** | proctor |
| **IRONMONGER** | hardware store |

# J

| | |
|---|---|
| **JAB** | shot |

| U.K. | U.S.A. |
|---|---|
| **JACK-DAW** | small crow |
| **JANNOCK** (dialect) | honest, genuine |
| **JEMMY** | jimmy |
| **JERRY** | chamber pot |
| **JIGGERY POKERY** | underhand scheming |
| **JOBATION** | a lengthy reprimand |
| **JOCK** | Scottish person |
| **JOE BLOGGS** | John Doe |
| **JOINT OF MEAT** | roast |
| **JOSSER** | fellow |
| **JUDDER** (mechanical) | vibrate or shake violently |
| **JUG** | pitcher |
| **JUGGED HARE** | rabbit stew |
| **JUGGERNAUT** | very large and heavy truck |
| **JUMBLE SALE** | used goods collected and sold, usually for charity |
| **JUMPED QUEUE** | cut in line |
| **JUMPER** | pullover, sweater |
| **JUNCTION (ROAD)** | intersection |
| **JUNIOR SCHOOL** | primary school (ages 7-11) |

# K

| | |
|---|---|
| **KECKS** | trousers |
| **KEEP YOUR PECKER UP** | maintain your courage |

| U.K. | U.S.A. |
|---|---|
| **KEN** (Sc.) | know, be acquainted with |
| **KENNEL** | dog house |
| **KENSPECKLE** | conspicuous |
| **KERB** | curb (edge of road) |
| **KERFUFFLE** | fuss, commotion |
| **KHAZI** | toilet |
| **KICK ONE'S HEELS** | to wait around |
| **KILLNER JAR** | ball/mason jar |
| **KIOSK** (phone) | booth |
| **KIOSK** (news) | stand |
| **KIP** | sleep |
| **KIPPER** | smoked herring |
| **KIRBY GRIP** | bobby pin |
| **KIRK** (Sc.) | church |
| **KISSING GATE** | gate allowing people through but not livestock |
| **KIT** (sports) | uniform |
| **KIT BAG** | soldier's duffel bag |
| **KITE MARK** | official mark indicating goods approved by British Standard Institution |
| **KNACKERED** | tired, worn-out |
| **KNACKER'S YARD** | place where old horses are slaughtered |
| **KNACKERS** (slang) | testicles, nuts, rocks |
| **KNEES UP** | lively dance party |
| **KNICKERS** | women's panties |

| U.K. | U.S.A. |
|---|---|
| **KNICKERS IN A TWIST** | panties in a wad |
| **KNOCKING SHOP** | brothel |
| **KNOCK UP** | wake up |

# L

| U.K. | U.S.A. |
|---|---|
| **L PLATE** | plate on a vehicle indicating student driver |
| **LABEL** | tag |
| **LADDER** (hosiery) | run |
| **LADYBIRD** | ladybug |
| **LARDER** | pantry |
| **LASHINGS** | plenty, an abundance |
| **LAST POST** | taps |
| **LAY ABOUT** | loafer |
| **LAY BY** | designated places for vehicles to pull over |
| **LEAD** | leash |
| **LEADER/LEADING ARTICLE** | main editorial/commentary |
| **LEADER** (orchestra) | concertmaster |
| **LEATHERJACKET** | harvestman grub |
| **LEFT LUGGAGE** | baggage room |
| **LEMON CURD** | spread made from eggs, butter, lemons, and sugar |

| U.K. | U.S.A. |
|---|---|
| **LENDING LIBRARY** | public library |
| **LET** | lease, rent |
| **LETTER BOX** | mailbox |
| **LEVANT** | to abscond with debt unpaid |
| **LEVEL CROSSING** | grade/railroad crossing |
| **LIBERTY BOAT** | boat carrying sailors ashore on leave |
| **LIBERTY BODICE** | closefitting women's undergarment |
| **LICENSED VICTUALLER** | innkeeper with a liquor license |
| **LIFT** | elevator |
| **LIGHTING UP TIME** | time when cars must switch on headlights |
| **LIKE THE CLAPPERS** | noisily, with gusto |
| **LIMITED/LTD.** | Incorporated/Inc. |
| **LINO** | linoleum |
| **LIP SALVE** | chapstick |
| **LIQUID PARAFFIN** | odorless, tasteless, mild laxative |
| **LIVER SAUSAGE** | liverwurst |
| **LOCAL (THE)** | tavern, neighborhood pub |
| **LOCH** (Sc.) | lake |
| **LOCK UP** | shop or garage (without living quarters) |
| **LODGER** | boarder |

| U.K. | U.S.A. |
|---|---|
| **LOLLIPOP LADY/MAN** | school crossing guard |
| **LOLLOP** | ungainly walk |
| **LONG CHALK (BY A)** | by a long shot, by far |
| **LOO** | bathroom, restroom |
| **LOOSE COVER** | slip cover |
| **LORD MUCK** | high-muck-a-muck |
| **LORRY** | truck, vehicle for carrying large goods |
| **LOSE MARKS** | count off |
| **LOUD HAILER** | bull horn |
| **LOUNGE SUIT** | business suit |
| **LUCERNE** | alfalfa/fodder |
| **LUCKY DIP** | grab bag |
| **LUG-HOLE** (slang) | ear |
| **LUM** (Sc.) | chimney |
| **LUNCHEON VOUCHER** | given to employees as part of pay and exchangeable for meals at many restaurants |
| **LURCHER** | a cross between a sheepdog and a greyhound |
| **LUTINE BELL** | bell rung at Lloyd's of London to announce the loss of a ship |

# M

| U.K. | U.S.A. |
|------|--------|
| **MAC, MACK** | mackintosh coat |
| **MACARONI-CHEESE** | macaroni and cheese |
| **MADEIRA CAKE** | rich, sweet sponge cake |
| **MAD ON** | crazy about |
| **MAINS** | power in the building |
| **MAINS LEAD** | outlet plug, adaptor |
| **MAINS RAZOR** | electric razor |
| **MAIZE COB** | corn on the cob |
| **MAKE A MEAL OF IT** | exaggerate |
| **MANUAL** (auto) | stick shift |
| **MARCHING ORDERS** | walking papers, dismissal |
| **MARKET GARDEN** | truck farm |
| **MARMITE** | spread made from essence of yeast and beef broth |
| **MARRAM GRASS** | dune grass |
| **MARROW** (vegetable) | squash |
| **MATCH** (soccer) | game |
| **MATE** | buddy |
| **MATELOT** | sailor |
| **MATHS** | math |
| **MAUNDY MONEY** | minted silver coins given to the poor by the reigning monarch on Maundy Thurs. |
| **MERCER** | dealer in textiles, e.g. silks |
| **MERRY DANCERS** | Aurora Borealis |
| **METHS** (see below) | |
| **METHYLATED SPIRITS** | denatured alcohol |

| U.K. | U.S.A. |
|---|---|
| MEWS | courtyard stables, often converted into dwellings |
| MILK FLOAT | light truck (usually electric) for delivering milk |
| MINCED MEAT/BEEF | hamburger meat, ground beef |
| MINCER | meat grinder |
| "MIND YOUR P'S AND Q'S" | "Be careful to be polite" |
| MIZZLE | to run away |
| MOCKERS | bad luck |
| MOGGIE | cat |
| MOIDER/MOITHER | confuse, worry, pester |
| MOKE | donkey |
| MONEY FOR JAM/OLD ROPE | profit for little effort |
| MOOR | open land |
| MOT (MINISTRY OF TRANSPORT) TEST | road safety test for vehicles |
| MOTHER'S DAY | fourth Sunday in Lent |
| MOTORING | driving |
| MOTORWAY | freeway |
| MOVE HOUSE | move |
| MRS. MOP | cleaning woman/housemaid |
| MUCK IN | get along with |
| MUCKING ABOUT | messing/horsing around |
| MUD GUARD | fender |

| U.K. | U.S.A. |
|---|---|
| **MUG** | gullible person |
| **MUGGINS** | one who lets him/herself be burdened |

# N

| U.K. | U.S.A. |
|---|---|
| **NAAFI** | PX |
| **NAIL VARNISH** | nail polish |
| **NANCY/NANCY BOY** | effeminate male/homosexual |
| **NANNY** | child's nurse |
| **NAPPER** | head |
| **NAPPY** | diaper |
| **NARK (COPPER)** (Sc.) | informer (police), stool pigeon |
| **NARK** | to annoy, make angry |
| **NATIONAL TRUST** | historic and natural beauty preservation organization |
| **NASTY BIT/PIECE OF WORK** | contemptible person |
| **NATTER** | talk, grumble |
| **NAVVY** | laborer on roads, railway |
| **NEARSIDE** (vehicle) | passenger side |
| **NEAR THE KNUCKLE** | somewhat indecent |
| **NEAT** (drink) | straight |
| **NEB** | bill, beak, tip |
| **NEEDLE MATCH** | rival match |

| U.K. | U.S.A. |
|---|---|
| NEEP (Sc.) | turnip |
| NET CURTAINS | sheer curtains, under-drapes |
| NEVER NEVER (THE) | installment plan |
| NEWMARKET (card game) | Michigan |
| NEWSAGENT | newsdealer/newstand |
| NICKER | one pound sterling |
| NIFF | a smell/stink |
| NIL | no score, zip |
| 999 | 911 |
| NINETEEN TO THE DOZEN | rapidly, very quickly |
| NIPPER | young boy or girl |
| NIPPY | agile, nimble, swift, can also mean cold |
| NOB | wealthy person |
| NOBBLE | tamper with racehorse to prevent its winning |
| NOD IS AS GOOD AS A WINK TO A BLIND HORSE | an expression about someone who refuses to take a hint |
| NOG | strong beer |
| NOSH | food (n.)/eat (v.) |
| NOSH UP | feast, large meal |
| NOT A FULL SHILLING | mentally deficient |
| NOT HALF | very much |
| NOT ON YOUR NELLY | not on your life |
| NOTICE BOARD | bulletin board |

| U.K. | U.S.A. |
|------|--------|
| NOUGHT | zero |
| NOUGHTS & CROSSES | tic-tac-toe |
| NUMBER PLATE | license plate |
| NURSING HOME | private hospital |
| NUTTER | crazy person |

# O

| | |
|------|--------|
| "O" LEVELS | "ordinary" high school exams |
| O.A.P. (Old Age Pensioner) | senior citizen |
| ODDS AND SODS | miscellaneous people/things |
| OFF COLOUR | feeling ill |
| OFF CUT | remnant |
| OFF LICENCE | liquor store |
| OFF PUTTING | disconcerting, repellent |
| OFF SIDE (vehicle) | driver's side |
| OFF THE PEG | off the rack |
| OFF THE RAILS | acting strangely or irresponsibly |
| OLD BILL | police |
| OLD BOY | alumnus |
| OLD LAG | hardened criminal |

| U.K. | U.S.A. |
|---|---|
| OLD SCHOOL TIE | upper class solidarity |
| OLD SWEAT | experienced person, old soldier |
| O.N.O (OR NEAR OFFER) | O.B.O. (or best offer) |
| ON THE MIKE | idling, being lazy |
| OPERATING THEATRE | operating room |
| OPPO | friend, colleague |
| OPPOSITION (THE) | main parliamentary party not in office |
| OPTIC | measuring device attached to liquor/wine bottle necks |
| ORANGE SQUASH | orange drink |
| ORBITAL | beltway |
| ORRA (Sc.) | extra, odd |
| OUTSIDE BROADCAST | broadcast on location |
| OVEN CLOTH/GLOVES | potholders/gloves |
| OVERDRESS | jumper |
| OVERTAKE | pass |
| O.V.N.O. | Or Very Near Offer |
| OXTER (Sc.) | armpit |

# P

| | |
|---|---|
| P.A.Y.E. (PAY AS YOU EARN) | income tax deducted from salary |

| U.K. | U.S.A. |
|---|---|
| **PACK** (of cards) | deck |
| **PACK UP** | stop working, break down |
| **PADDY** | tantrum, fit |
| **PANDA CAR** | police patrol car |
| **PANTECHNICON** | furniture removal van |
| **PANTOMIME (PANTO)** | Christmas show with singing, dancing, and slapstick comedy, usually with audience participation and normally adapted from fairy tales. |
| **PANTS/UNDERPANTS** | men's underwear |
| **PARAFFIN** | kerosene |
| **PARALYTIC** | very drunk |
| **PARCEL** | package |
| **PARKY** | chilly (weather) |
| **PASS OUT** (military) | finish training |
| **PASTY** | crusted pie |
| **PATCH (GOOD OR BAD)** | period, stage |
| **PATIENCE** (card game) | solitaire |
| **PAVEMENT** | sidewalk |
| **PAWKY** (Sc.) | shrewd, having a dry humor |
| **PAY PACKET** | pay envelope |
| **PECKISH** | slightly hungry |
| **PELICAN CROSSING** | lighted pedestrian crossing |
| **PELMET** | valance |
| **PENNY DREADFUL** | cheap storybook/magazine |

| U.K. | U.S.A. |
| --- | --- |
| PEPPER POT | pepper shaker |
| PERAMBULATOR/PRAM | baby carriage |
| PERMANENT WAY | rail or tram tracks |
| PERRY | hard cider made from pears |
| PERSPEX® | plexiglass® |
| PETROL | gasoline, gas |
| PETROL BOMB | Molotov cocktail |
| PICTURES | movies |
| PIGEON PAIR | boy and girl twins |
| PIG'S EAR | mess, failure |
| PILLAR BOX | mailbox, mail drop |
| PILLOCK | stupid person |
| PINAFORE | apron |
| PINK | young salmon |
| PINNY | apron |
| PIP (THE) | depressed, annoyed |
| PIPPED AT THE POST | beaten (in a race) |
| PIPS | seeds, pits |
| PISSED | drunk |
| PITCH (sports) | field |
| PLANT (billiards) | combination shot |
| PLASTER | band-aid |
| PLIMSOLLS/PUMPS | canvas sports shoes, Keds |
| PLOUGHMAN'S LUNCH | meal of bread, cheese, etc. |
| PLUS-FOURS/TWOS | knickers/knickerbockers |
| PO-FACED | solemn, humorless |
| POINT DUTY | traffic duty |
| POLICE INSPECTOR | police captain |

| U.K. | U.S.A. |
|---|---|
| **POLONECK** (sweater) | turtleneck |
| **POLONY** | bologna |
| **POLYSTYRENE** | styrofoam |
| **POMFRET/PONTEFRACT** | |
| **CAKE** | small, flat, round licorice candy |
| **PONCE** | pimp; move effeminately |
| **PONTOON** (cards) | blackjack, 21 |
| **PONY** | twenty-five pounds sterling |
| **POOFTER** | male homosexual, effeminate man |
| **POP** | hock, pawn |
| **POP ROUND** | come to visit |
| **POPPET** | small dainty person, term of endearment |
| **POSITIVE** | |
| **DISCRIMINATION** | affirmative action |
| **POST** | mail |
| **POSTAGE** | shipping |
| **POST CODE/POSTAL CODE** | zip code |
| **POSTAL ORDER** | money order |
| **POSY** | small bunch of flowers |
| **POTABLE** | drinkable |
| **POT HOLER** | spelunker, cave explorer |
| **POTTED MEAT** | head cheese |
| **POTTER** | dawdle, loiter |
| **POTTY** | silly, slightly crazy |

| U.K. | U.S.A. |
|---|---|
| POWER POINT | electrical outlet |
| PRAM (PERAMBULATOR) | baby carriage |
| PRANG | crash (vehicle) |
| PREFECT (school) | student monitor |
| PREP | school homework |
| PRESS MARK (library) | call number |
| PRESS STUDS/POPPERS | snaps |
| PRIVATE PATIENT | patient not under the National Health Service |
| PRIVY PURSE | the monarchy's allowance |
| PROM | concert |
| PROSY | commonplace, tedious, dull |
| PUBLICAN | manager/owner of a tavern |
| PUBLIC CONVENIENCE | public restroom/toilets |
| PUBLIC SCHOOL | private school |
| PUDDING | dessert |
| PUNCH UP | fight or brawl |
| PUNNET | small basket for fruit |
| PUNTER | customer, specifically of a prostitute; also a gambler |
| PURCHASE TAX | sales tax |
| PURL (colloq.) | turn upside down |
| PURLER | fall head first |
| PURSE | change purse, coin purse |
| PUSH CHAIR | stroller |
| PUT A SOCK IN IT | shut up, be quiet |
| PUTTY MEDAL | fit reward for small service |

| U.K. | U.S.A. |
|------|--------|

# Q

| | |
|------|--------|
| **QUARENDEN** | red apple |
| **QUARTER DAYS** | Mar. 25, Jun. 24, Sep. 29, and Dec. 25 |
| **QUARTER-LIGHT** (vehicle) | wing window |
| **QUAVER** | an eighth note |
| **QUEER ONE'S PITCH** | upset one's plans |
| **QUEUE** | a line |
| **QUEUE UP** | stand in line |
| **QUEUE JUMP** | cut in line |
| **QUID** | one pound sterling |
| **QUIDS IN** | made a profit |
| **QUIFF** | curl of hair on forehead |

# R

| | |
|------|--------|
| **RACHMANISM** | landlord's exploitation of slum tenants |
| **RAG** | prank |
| **RAG AND BONE MAN** | itinerant dealer in old clothes and other goods, junkman |
| **RAG DAY** | annual comic day held by students to raise money for charity |

| U.K. | U.S.A. |
|---|---|
| **RAMP** | swindle, usually by overcharging |
| **RASHER** (bacon) | slice |
| **RATES** | property taxes |
| **RATING** | non-commissioned sailor |
| **RAWLPLUGS** | anchors |
| **RECORDED DELIVERY** | certified mail, return receipt |
| **RED CAP** | military policeman |
| **REDD** (Sc.) | clear up, tidy, settle |
| **REDUNDANT (MADE)** | laid off work, riffed |
| **REGISTRY OFFICE** | local government office that conducts marriages |
| **REMEMBRANCE DAY** | Veteran's Day |
| **REMAND CENTRE** | detention center |
| **RETURN** (ticket) | round trip |
| **RETURNING OFFICER** | official who announces election results |
| **REVERSE CHARGES** | call collect |
| **REVERSING LIGHTS** | backing up lights |
| **RHINE** | a large open ditch |
| **RHINO** | money, cash |
| **RICK** (neck or back) | sprain, twist |
| **RING, RING UP** | call |
| **RING ROAD** | belt highway |
| **ROCKET** | reprimand |
| **ROLLER BLIND** | window shade |
| **RORTY** | enjoyable |

| U.K. | U.S.A. |
|---|---|
| **ROTA** | roster |
| **ROTOVATOR** | power driven soil tiller |
| **ROUNDABOUT** | traffic circle; also a merry-go-round |
| **ROUNDERS** | game similar to baseball |
| **ROUND TRIP** | circular journey |
| **ROUP** | sell at auction |
| **ROW** | argument |
| **ROWAN TREE** | mountain ash |
| **ROYAL MAIL** | U.S. Postal Service |
| **RUBBER** | eraser |
| **RUBBISH TIP** | trash dump |
| **RUCTION** (colloq.) | disturbance, tumult |
| **RUDDY** (slang) | bloody, damned |
| **RUGGER** | rugby |
| **RUM** (person) | odd, strange |
| **RUNDALE/RUNRIG** | joint occupation of land |
| **RUNNER BEAN** | string bean |
| **RUNNING KNOT** | slip knot |
| **RUN TO** | afford |
| **RUN UP** | prelude |

# S

| | |
|---|---|
| **SAIL CLOSE TO THE WIND** | almost get into trouble |

| U.K. | U.S.A. |
|---|---|
| SALAD CREAM | salad dressing, like Miracle Whip® |
| SALOON CAR | sedan |
| SALT CELLAR | salt shaker |
| SAND MARTIN | bank swallow |
| SANITARY TOWEL | sanitary napkin/pad |
| SAPPER | soldier with the Royal Engineers |
| SARNIE | sandwich |
| SASSENACH | Scot's term for English person |
| SAUSAGE ROLL | sausage meat wrapped in flaky pastry |
| SCAREDY CAT | fraidy cat |
| SCARPER | to run away |
| SCATTY | harebrained |
| SCOTCH EGG | hard-boiled egg covered in sausage meat |
| SCOUSE | native of Liverpool or the Liverpudlian dialect |
| SCRAMBLES (motorcycle) | motorcross |
| SCRIMSHANK | to shirk duty |
| SCUNNER | to feel sick; a strong dislike |
| SCUPPER | sink a ship, spoil plans |
| SECATEURS | pruning shears/clippers |
| SELLOTAPE | Scotch tape |
| SEMIBREVE | whole note |
| SEMI-DETACHED | duplex |

| U.K. | U.S.A. |
|---|---|
| **SEMIQUAVER** | sixteenth note |
| **SEMOLINA** | cream of wheat |
| **SEND UP** | satirize, ridicule |
| **SERVIETTE** | table napkin |
| **SETTEE** | loveseat |
| **SHAG** | copulate |
| **SHAW** | small wood, thicket |
| **SHIELING** (Sc.) | hut used by shepherds/ sportsmen |
| **SHIPPON** | cattle shed |
| **SHOOTING BRAKE** | station wagon |
| **SHOOT THE MOON** | move house at night to avoid paying rent |
| **SHOPPING PRECINCT** | shopping mall |
| **SHORT** | cocktail |
| **SHORT A SHINGLE** | feeble-minded |
| **SHORT LIST** | list of final choices |
| **SHOWER** | contemptible/unpleasant person(s) |
| **SHUFTI** | a look (at a thing) |
| **SIDEBOARDS** | sideburns |
| **SIGNAL BOX** (rail) | signal tower |
| **SIGN POST** | street sign |
| **SILENCER** (auto) | muffler |
| **SILLER** (Sc.) | money |
| **SILLY BUGGER** | foolish person |
| **SILVER PAPER** | aluminum foil |

| U.K. | U.S.A. |
|---|---|
| **SILVER SIDE** | cut of beef |
| **SIMNEL CAKE** | rich fruit cake |
| **SINGLE** | one-way ticket |
| **SINGLET** | sleeveless undershirt |
| **SISTER (WARD)** | senior nurse |
| **SKELP** | hit, beat, spank |
| **SKID CHAINS** | snow chains |
| **SKILLY** | thin soup |
| **SKIP** | dumpster |
| **SKIRTING BOARD** | baseboard |
| **SKIVE** | avoid work |
| **SKIVVY** | a female domestic servant |
| **SLAP & TICKLE** | boisterous, amorous amusement |
| **SLATE** | criticize severely |
| **SLEEPERS** | railroad ties |
| **SLEEPING PARTNER** | silent partner |
| **SLEEPING POLICEMEN** | speed bumps |
| **SLIP ROAD** | ramp |
| **SLOSH** | to hit |
| **SLOSHED** | drunk, smashed |
| **SMALLS** | underwear |
| **SMASHING** | first rate, excellent |
| **SNAFFLE** | to steal |
| **SNECK** | door latch |
| **SNIGGER** | snicker |
| **SNOGGING** | making out |

| U.K. | U.S.A. |
|---|---|
| SOD (vulgar) | bastard; short for sodomy |
| SOD-ALL | nothing |
| SOD OFF (vulgar) | go away |
| SOLICITOR | lawyer, attorney |
| SONSY (Sc.) | cheerful; buxom |
| SORT | mend |
| SPANNER | wrench |
| SPECIAL CONSTABLE | part-time policeman |
| SPEECH DAY | annual prize giving day |
| SPEND A PENNY | go to the toilet |
| SPINNEY | small wood |
| SPIV | con man |
| SPONGE BAG | toiletries bag |
| SPOT | zit |
| SPOT ON | right on |
| SPOTTED DICK | plum duff (see duff) |
| SQUADDY | private soldier, recruit |
| STALLS | orchestra seats |
| STANDARD LAMP | floor lamp |
| STANDING ORDER | direct/preauthorized debit |
| STANNARY | tin mine |
| STARKERS | completely naked |
| STARTERS | appetizers |
| STEPS | ladder |
| STICKY BUN | sweet roll with frosting |
| STICKY WICKET | sticky situation |
| STONE (weight) | fourteen pounds |

| U.K. | U.S.A. |
|---|---|
| **STONES** | pits, seeds |
| **STOP AT HOME** | stay at home |
| **STOPPED UP** | bunged up |
| **STRATH** (Sc.) | wide valley |
| **STROLLER** | push chair |
| **STROPPY** | bad tempered, awkward |
| **STUMER** | worthless money, fraud |
| **STUMP UP** | pay up |
| **SUBTOPIA** | urban sprawl |
| **SUBWAY** | underground pedestrian walkway |
| **SULTANAS** | golden raisins |
| **SUMP** (auto) | oil pan |
| **SUN BLIND** | window awning |
| **SURGERY** (doctor's) | office (doctor's or dentist's) |
| **SURGICAL SPIRITS** | rubbing alcohol |
| **SUS OUT** | figure out; check over |
| **SUSPENDERS** | garters |
| **SUSPENDER BELT** | garter belt |
| **SWALLOW DIVE** | swan dive |
| **SWEDE** | rutabaga |
| **SWEET** | dessert; a candy |
| **SWEET SHOP** | candy store |
| **SWINE FEVER** | hog cholera |
| **SWINGS AND ROUNDABOUTS** | break even; "six of one, half a dozen of the other" |

| U.K. | U.S.A. |
|---|---|
| **SWING THE LEAD** | malinger |
| **SWIPES** | inferior beer |
| **SWISS ROLL** | jelly roll |
| **SWITCHBACK** | roller coaster; road with alternating ups and downs |
| **SWIZZ** | to cheat, swindle |
| **SWOT** | study in depth for exams |

# T

| | |
|---|---|
| **TA** | thank you |
| **TABLE** | submit for discussion, propose |
| **TAIL BACK** (traffic) | back up |
| **TAKE A FANCY TO** | take a liking to |
| **TAKE-AWAY** | take-out |
| **TANNOY** | public address system |
| **TAP** | faucet |
| **TARTED UP** | dressed up |
| **TATTOO** | outdoor military display or march |
| **TATTY** | shabby |
| **TAXI RANK** | taxi stand |
| **TEA CAKE** | sweet bun with raisins |
| **TEA TOWEL** | dish towel, kitchen towel |

49

| U.K. | U.S.A. |
|---|---|
| **TEDDY BOY** | a youth preferring the Edwardian style of dress (a 1950's fad) |
| **TELLY** | television |
| **TEN-A-PENNY** | dime a dozen |
| **TENNER** | ten-pound note |
| **TENPINS** | bowling |
| **TENTER** | person who looks after things; watchdog |
| **TERRACE HOUSES** | row houses |
| **THWAITE** | some wild land made arable |
| **TICK** | credit |
| **TICK** | a check mark |
| **TICKETY BOO** | all right, hunky dory |
| **TICK OVER** (vehicle) | idling speed |
| **TICK TACK** | manual signaling used by racecourse bookmakers |
| **TIED COTTAGE** | occupied by tenant only while working for the owner |
| **TIED HOUSE** | pub only allowed to sell a particular brewer's liquor |
| **TIGHTS** | panty hose |
| **TILL** | cash register |
| **TIME TABLE** | schedule |
| **TIP LORRY** | dump truck |
| **TITCH** | small person |
| **TITFER** | hat |

| U.K. | U.S.A. |
|---|---|
| **TOAD IN THE HOLE** | sausages in Yorkshire pudding |
| **TOE-RAG** | annoying person, tramp |
| **TOFF** | upper class man, a dandy |
| **TOFFEE NOSED** | snobbish, pretentious |
| **TOMATO SAUCE** | ketchup |
| **TOMMY** | a British soldier |
| **TON** | speed of 100 mph; score of 100 |
| **TOO CLEVER BY HALF** | to smart for his own good |
| **TOP DRAWER** | of the highest social position |
| **TOP HOLE** | first rate |
| **TOPPING** | excellent |
| **TOP UP** (drink) | refill |
| **TORCH** | flashlight |
| **TOT** | jigger |
| **TOTTER** | junkman |
| **TOWPATH** | path alongside a river/canal |
| **TRACKSUIT** | sweatsuit |
| **TRAFFIC WARDEN** | parking meter patrol person, sometimes assists police in traffic duty |
| **TRAILER** (film) | preview (movie) |
| **TRAM** | streetcar |
| **TRANSPORT CAFE** | truck stop |
| **TRAVELLING RUG** | lap robe, lap blanket |
| **TREACLE (BLACK)** | molasses |

51

| U.K. | U.S.A. |
|---|---|
| **TRICKEY WICKET** | sticky situation |
| **TRIFLE** | a dessert of sponge cake, fruit, wine, jello, custard, cream |
| **TRILBY** | fedora |
| **TRIPPER** | vacationer (especially for a day) |
| **TRUG** | shallow, wooden garden basket |
| **TRUNCHEON** | night stick |
| **TRUNK ROAD** | main highway |
| **TUBE** | subway |
| **TUCK IN** | eat heartily |
| **TUCK SHOP** | candy store (usually at a school) |
| **TURF ACCOUNTANT** | bookie |
| **TURN UPS** | pant cuffs |
| **TUPPENNY HA'PENNY** | unimportant, worthless, two bit |
| **TWEE** | dainty, quaint |
| **TWICER** | double dealer, cheat |
| **TWIT** | jerk |
| **TYKE** | Yorkshireman; a rascal |
| **TYRE** | tire |

# U

| U.K. | U.S.A. |
|---|---|
| **UNIT TRUST** | Municipal Investment Trust |
| **UPPER CIRCLE** | first balcony |

# V

| | |
|---|---|
| **VACUUM FLASK** | Thermos |
| **VERGER** | church official |
| **VEST** | undershirt |
| **VET** | to examine and check for accuracy or suitability |
| **VICAR** | pastor |

# W

| | |
|---|---|
| **WAD** | sandwich |
| **WAFFLE** | to speak or write imprecisely |
| **WAG** | to be truant, to play hooky |
| **WAISTCOAT** | vest |
| **WALTZER** (ride) | tilt a whirl |
| **WARDER** | prison guard |
| **WASH UP** | clean dishes, etc. |
| **WATERBOATMAN** | waterbug |
| **WELLIES** | Wellington boots waterproof |

| U.K. | U.S.A. |
|---|---|
| WELSH DRESSER | hutch |
| WENDY HOUSE | child's playhouse |
| WHACKED | tired out |
| WHACKING | huge |
| WASHING-UP POWDER | detergent |
| WHIP ROUND | collection of money from a group of people |
| WHIT SUNDAY | seventh Sun. after Easter |
| WHITE COFFEE | coffee with cream |
| WIDE BOY | quick witted but dishonest person |
| WIMPY (colloq.) | hamburger in a plain bun |
| WINCEYETTE | type of lightweight flannelette |
| WIND CHEATER | wind breaker |
| WINDLESTRAW | old dry grass |
| WINDSCREEN | windshield |
| WIND YOU UP | tease |
| WINE GUM | gum drop |
| WINKLE-PICKERS | long, very pointed shoes |
| WITTER ON | speak at length about trivial matters |
| WONKY | shaky, unreliable |
| WOTCHER? | how are you? |
| WREN (Women's Navy) | WAVE |
| WRITE OFF (vehicle) | to completely wreck, total |
| WYND (Sc.) | alley, narrow street |

| U.K. | U.S.A. |
|------|--------|

# Y

| | |
|------|--------|
| **YANKEE** (betting) | bet on four or more horses to win or place in different races |
| **YOB** | lout, hooligan |
| **YONKS** | very long time |
| **YORKS** | abbreviation for Yorkshire |
| **YORKSHIRE PUDDING** | popover-type biscuit |
| **YOU LOT** | you guys |

# Z

| | |
|------|--------|
| **ZEBRA CROSSING** | pedestrian crossing |
| **ZED** | Z |
| **ZIP-FASTENER** | zipper |

# U.S.A.
# to
# U.K.

## AMERICAN WORDS AND
## EXPRESSIONS AND
## BRITISH COUNTERPARTS

| U.S.A. | U.K. |
|---|---|

# A

| | |
|---|---|
| **A LA MODE** | served with ice cream |
| **ABSORBENT COTTON** | cotton wool |
| **ACCLIMATED** | acclimatised |
| **AFFIRMATIVE ACTION** | positive discrimination |
| **AIRDROME/PLANE** | aerodrome/plane |
| **ALUMNI/AE** | former pupils (male/female) |
| **ALUMNUS** | old boy |
| **AMBULANCE CHASER** | lawyer who encourages clients to sue for damages after an accident |
| **ANCHORS** | rawlplugs |
| **ANTENNA** | aerial |
| **APARTMENT** | flat |
| **APARTMENT BUILDING** | block of flats |
| **APPETIZER** | starter |
| **ARROYO** | stream, gully |
| **ASHCAN** | dustbin |
| **ASS** | backside, arse, bum |

# B

| | |
|---|---|
| **BABYSITTER** | child-minder |
| **BAD MANNERS** | bad form |

| U.S.A. | U.K. |
|---|---|
| **BAKED POTATO** | jacket potato |
| **BALL JAR** | Killner jar |
| **BALLPARK** | baseball ground |
| **BALLPARK FIGURE** | estimate, approximate amount |
| **BAND-AID** | elastoplast |
| **BANGS** | hair fringe |
| **BANG UP** | first class, terrific |
| **BANK SHOT** (billiards) | double |
| **BARETTE** | hair clip |
| **BARF** | vomit |
| **BARKEEP** | bar tender |
| **BASEBOARD** | skirting board |
| **BAZOO** | mouth |
| **BEAN COUNTER** | accountant |
| **BELLHOP/BELLPERSON** | page |
| **BELL PEPPER** | green pepper |
| **BELLY UP** | business failure, shut down |
| **BELT HIGHWAY** | ring road |
| **BENNY** | overcoat |
| **BILK** | swindle |
| **BILL** | banknote |
| **BILLBOARD** | hoarding |
| **BILLFOLD** | wallet |
| **BIRD DOG** | retriever |
| **BISCUIT** | a soft unsweetened roll |
| **BITCH** (slang) | complain |

| U.S.A. | U.K. |
| --- | --- |
| **BITCHIN'** | great |
| **BITTERSWEET CHOCOLATE** | plain chocolate |
| **BLACKJACK** | cosh |
| **BLEACHERS** | grandstand seats, usually unsheltered |
| **BLIND** | hide (observation) |
| **BLOOPER** | blunder, usually in public |
| **BLOWS** (it blows) | it's bad |
| **BLUE LAWS** | Sunday trading laws |
| **BOARDWALK** | raised walkway, usually by the beach |
| **BOBBY PIN** | hair grip, kirby grip |
| **BOLOGNA** | polony |
| **BOMB** | a failure, disaster |
| **BONE UP** | to study |
| **BONER** | silly idea, blooper, error |
| **BONER** (slang) | erection |
| **BOOKMOBILE** | mobile library |
| **BOONDOCKS/BOONIES** | isolated countryside |
| **BOONDOGGLE** | trivial or unnecessary work |
| **BOOTY** | bottom, buttocks |
| **BOXCAR** (rail) | enclosed goods wagon |
| **BROIL** | grill |
| **BRONX CHEER** | blow a raspberry |
| **BUG** | insect |
| **BULL HORN** | loud hailer |

| U.S.A. | U.K. |
|---|---|
| BULL PEN | baseball pitcher's practice area |
| BUMMER | unpleasant experience |
| BUNCO/BUNKO | swindle |
| BUNK | nonsense |
| BUNS/BUTT (slang) | bum, buttocks |
| BURGLARIZE | burgle |
| BURRO | small donkey |
| BUSBOY/BUSPERSON | waiter's assistant |
| BUSINESS SUIT | lounge suit |
| BUSS | kiss |
| BUSY (phone) | engaged (line) |
| BUTTE | solitary hill or mountain |
| BUTTONWOOD/SYCAMORE | plane tree |

# C

| | |
|---|---|
| CABANA | beach shelter |
| CABOOSE (rail) | guard's van |
| CALABOOSE | prison |
| CALL (phone) | ring |
| CALL COLLECT | reverse charges |
| CALL NUMBER (library) | press mark |
| CANDIED FRUIT | crystallized fruit |
| CANDY | sweets, chocolate |
| CANDY STORE | sweet shop |

| U.S.A. | U.K. |
|---|---|
| **CAREEN** | career |
| **CAR HOP** | waiter at a drive-in restaurant |
| **CARNIVAL** | fun fair |
| **CARRY-OUT** | take away |
| **CASH REGISTER** | till |
| **CATERCORNER/ CATTYCORNER** | diagonally opposite |
| **CATNIP** | cat-mint |
| **CATTAIL** | bullrush |
| **CERTIFIED MAIL** | recorded delivery |
| **CHANGE/COIN PURSE** | purse |
| **CHAPSTICK** | lip salve |
| **CHARLEY HORSE** | cramps (arms, legs) |
| **CHECK** (mark) | tick |
| **CHECK** (payment) | cheque |
| **CHECK** (restaurant) | bill |
| **CHECK-IN** | book-in |
| **CHECKERS** | draughts |
| **CHECKROOM** | cloakroom |
| **CHICKADEE** | titmouse |
| **CHINCHBUG** | small insect that destroys grain, etc. |
| **CHIPPER** | cheerful |
| **CHIPS** (potato) | crisps |
| **CHOWDER** | fish stew or soup |
| **CINDER BLOCK** | breeze block |

| U.S.A. | U.K. |
|---|---|
| **CITY EDITOR** | editor dealing with local news |
| **CITY GOVERNMENT** | corporation |
| **CLOSET** | cupboard |
| **CLOSET** (clothes) | wardrobe |
| **CLOTHESPIN** | clothes-peg |
| **COLLAR, STAY AND BUTTON** | collar, stiffener and stud |
| **COLD COCK** | hit hard |
| **COMBINATION SHOT** (billiards) | plant |
| **COMFORTER** | eiderdown |
| **COMMERCIALS** | adverts |
| **CONDOMINIUM/CONDO** | privately owned/leased flat |
| **CONDUCTOR** (rail) | guard |
| **CONFECTIONER'S SUGAR** | icing sugar |
| **CONNECT** (phone) | put through |
| **CONNIPTION** (fit) | a fit of rage or hysteria, "throw a wobbler" |
| **CONSTRUCTION** | road works |
| **COOKIE** | biscuit (sweet) |
| **COOKIE SHEET** | baking tray |
| **COOKOUT** | barbeque |
| **CORNSTARCH** | corn flour |
| **COT** | camp bed |
| **COTTON CANDY** | candy floss |

| U.S.A. | U.K. |
|---|---|
| COUCH POTATO | T.V. addict, inactive person |
| COUNTER-CLOCKWISE | anti-clockwise |
| COUNT OFF | lose marks |
| COVER CHARGE | entrance fee |
| COW CHIP | cow pat |
| CRACKER | biscuit (unsweetened) |
| CRACK UP | laugh |
| CRAZY BONE | funny bone |
| CREAM OF WHEAT | semolina |
| CREEK | stream |
| CROSSING GUARD | lollipop lady/man |
| CRUD | filth |
| CRULLER | small doughnut/cake |
| CRY UNCLE | admit defeat |
| CUFFS (on pants) | turn-ups (on trousers) |
| CUPBOARD | kitchen cabinet |
| CURB | kerb |
| CURVE BALL | googly |
| CUSTOM-MADE | bespoke, made to measure |
| CUTE | attractive, quaint |
| CUT THE MUSTARD | meet required standard |
| CUTTING IN LINE | queue jumping |

# D

| | |
|---|---|
| DANDER | temper |

| U.S.A. | U.K. |
|---|---|
| **DANDY** | good |
| **DAVENPORT** | large sofa |
| **DEAD TO RIGHTS** | red-handed |
| **DEALERSHIP** | car manufacturer's franchise |
| **DECK** (cards) | pack |
| **DECK SHOES** | boat shoes |
| **DEEP SIX** | get rid of |
| **DELI** | delicatessen shop |
| **DENATURED ALCOHOL** | methylated spirits/meths |
| **DERBY HAT** | bowler hat |
| **DETOUR** | diversion |
| **DIAPER** | nappy |
| **DICTY** | stylish |
| **DIDDLY-SQUAT** | nothing |
| **DIDO** | prank, caper |
| **DIME STORE** | inexpensive store |
| **DINGBAT** | stupid person |
| **DINKY** | trifling |
| **DISHTOWEL** | tea towel |
| **DISORIENTED** | disorientated |
| **DITSY** | silly, stupid |
| **DIVIDED HIGHWAY** | dual carriageway |
| **DOCKET** | list of court cases |
| **DOGGIE BAG** | container provided by restaurants to take leftovers |
| **DOG'S AGE** | donkey's years |
| **DOOHICKEY** | small object |

| U.S.A. | U.K. |
|---|---|
| **DOWNTOWN** | town centre, city centre |
| **DRAFT (THE)** | conscription |
| **DRAPES** | curtains |
| **DRESSER** | chest of drawers |
| **DRUGSTORE** | chemist shop |
| **DRY GOODS STORE** | drapery |
| **DUCK SOUP** | easy task, money for jam |
| **DUDED UP** | dressed up |
| **DUFF** (slang) | buttocks |
| **DUMMY UP** | keep quiet |
| **DUMPSTER** | skip |
| **DUPLEX** | semi-detached property |

# E

| | |
|---|---|
| **EAT CROW** | submit to humiliation |
| **EDITORIAL** | leader |
| **EFFICIENCY** | self-catering apartment |
| **EGGPLANT** | aubergine |
| **ELECTRIC CORD** | flex |
| **ELEVATOR** | lift |
| **END OF YOUR ROPE** | end of your tether |
| **ENGLISH MUFFIN** | type of crumpet |
| **ENTREE** | main course of meal |
| **ESTATE TAX** | death duties |

| U.S.A. | U.K. |
|---|---|
| **F** | |
| **FACULTY** | staff |
| **FAG** | homosexual |
| **FAIR-HAIRED BOY** | blue-eyed boy |
| **FALL** | autumn |
| **FANNY** | buttocks, bottom |
| **FAUCET** | tap |
| **FEEB** | stupid person, idiot |
| **FEISTY** | aggressive |
| **FENDER** | bumper (car), mudguard (bike) |
| **FIELD HOCKEY** | hockey |
| **FINK** | nasty person, telltale |
| **FIRECRACKER** | banger |
| **FIRST BALCONY** | upper circle |
| **FIRST FLOOR** | ground floor |
| **FIXING TO** | preparing to |
| **FIXINGS** | meal accompaniments, trimmings |
| **FLACK** | publicity agent |
| **FLASHLIGHT** | torch |
| **FLAT PAINT** | emulsion |
| **FLATWARE** | cutlery |
| **FLIVVER** | cheap car or aeroplane |
| **FLOOR LAMP** | standard lamp |
| **FLOP HOUSE** | doss house |

| U.S.A. | U.K. |
|---|---|
| **FLUB** | botch, bungle |
| **FLUBDUB** | claptrap, bombastic language |
| **FLUID OUNCE (U.S.)** | 1.041 U.K. fluid ounces |
| **FLUNK** | fail |
| **FLUTIST** | flautist |
| **FLYER** | leaflet |
| **FOOSBALL** | table soccer |
| **FRAIDY CAT** | scaredy cat |
| **FRANKS** | short for frankfurters, hot dogs |
| **FREE SHIPPING** | carriage paid |
| **FREEWAY** | motorway |
| **FREIGHT/FREIGHT TRUCK** | goods/goods wagon |
| **FREIGHT ELEVATOR** | goods lift |
| **FRENCH FRIES** | chips |
| **FRESHMAN** | first year undergraduate |
| **FRIGATE** | large destroyer |
| **FRITZ (ON THE)** | out of order |
| **FRONT DESK** | reception |
| **FUN FAIR** | school or church bazaar |
| **FUNK** | strong smell |

# G

| | |
|---|---|
| **GABFEST** | long spell of talking |

| U.S.A. | U.K. |
|---|---|
| GAINER (FULL) | somersault |
| GALLON (U.S.) | 0.833 U.K. gallon |
| GARAGE SALE | house clearance sale |
| GARBAGE | rubbish |
| GARBAGE TRUCK/CAN | dustcart/bin |
| GARTER BELT | suspender belt |
| GARTERS | suspenders |
| GAS/GASOLINE | petrol |
| GAS STATION | petrol/filling station |
| GEAR/STICK SHIFT | gear lever |
| GET ON THE STICK | take hold of the situation |
| GIZMO | gadget |
| GOBBLEDYGOOK | jibberish |
| GOLDBRICK | shirker, lazy person |
| GOOF OFF | skive |
| GOOSE EGG (sports) | duck egg, no score |
| G.O.P. | Grand Old Party (Republican) |
| GOUGE | swindle, cheat |
| GRAB BAG | lucky dip |
| GRADE | class, form, year |
| GRADE CROSSING | level crossing |
| GRADE/GRAMMAR SCHOOL | junior school |
| GRANDSTANDING | playing to the gallery |
| GREASE MONKEY | mechanic |
| GREENBACK | U. S. banknote |

| U.S.A. | U.K. |
|---|---|
| **GRIDIRON** | American football or the field |
| **GRINDER** | hardworking student, type of sandwich |
| **GRIPSACK** | travelling bag/suitcase |
| **GROSS** | horrible, foul |
| **GROUND/GROUND WIRE** | earth/earthwire |
| **GROUND BEEF** | minced beef |
| **GRUBSTAKE** | investment in new enterprise, expecting a share of profits |
| **GULCH** | ravine, gully |
| **GUMBO** | spicy soup made with okra |
| **GUMSHOE** | galosh, detective |

# H

| U.S.A. | U.K. |
|---|---|
| **HABERDASHERY** | a men's clothing and furnishings shop |
| **HALF STAFF** | half-mast |
| **HAMBURGER BUN** | bap |
| **HAMBURGER MEAT** | minced beef |
| **HAND OFF** (sports) | to hand the ball to a teammate |
| **HAPPENSTANCE** | happens by chance |
| **HARD CANDY** | boiled sweets |

| U.S.A. | U.K. |
|---|---|
| **HARDSCRABBLE** | minimum return from maximum effort |
| **HARDWARE STORE** | ironmongers |
| **HARVESTMAN** | daddy longlegs |
| **HASH-SLINGER** | waiter/waitress |
| **HATCHECK PERSON** | cloakroom attendant |
| **HAUL/HAUL ASS** | to go fast |
| **HAVE A GANDER** | have a look |
| **HAZING** | bullying, humiliating |
| **HEAD** | toilet |
| **HEADCHEESE** | potted meat |
| **HEAD/VALVE JOB** (auto) | decoke |
| **HEATER** | handgun/firearm |
| **HEINIE** | bum, buttocks |
| **HEIST** | robbery |
| **HELLION** | mischievious, troublesome, usually a child |
| **HICK** | country bumpkin |
| **HICKEY** | love bite, also a pipe bender |
| **HIGH BALL** | whiskey and water with ice |
| **HIGHBINDER** | swindler or ruffian |
| **HIGH BOY** | tall boy |
| **HIGH-MUCK-A-MUCK** | Lord muck |
| **HIGH ROLLER** | big spender |
| **HIGH TAIL** | rush, get out fast |
| **HIKE** | raise |
| **HOBO** | tramp or wanderer |

| U.S.A. | U.K. |
|---|---|
| **HOCK/IN HOCK** | pawn/in debt |
| **HOCKEY** | ice hockey |
| **HOG CHOLERA** | swine fever |
| **HOG PEN** | pig sty |
| **HOKEY** | corny |
| **HOMELY** (person) | ugly, unattractive |
| **HOMEMAKER** | housewife |
| **HOMER** | home run in baseball |
| **HONCHO, HEAD HONCHO** | boss |
| **HOOCH** | alcoholic drink, usually illicit |
| **HOOD** (auto) | bonnet |
| **HOOEY** | nonsense |
| **HOOKY** (play) | truant |
| **HOOSEGOW** | prison |
| **HOOTERS** | breasts |
| **HOPE CHEST** | bottom drawer |
| **HORSE OPERA** | western film |
| **HORSING AROUND** | mucking about |
| **HOT DOG BUN** | bridge roll |
| **HUNDREDWEIGHT** | 100 pounds |
| **HUNK** | attractive man |
| **HUNKY-DORY** | fine, satisfactory |
| **HUSH PUPPY** | quick-fried maize bread |
| **HUTCH** | Welsh dresser |

| U.S.A. | U.K. |
|---|---|

# I

| | |
|---|---|
| **ICEBOX** | refrigerator |
| **ICE CREAM CONE** | ice cream cornet |
| **INCORPORATED/INC.** | Limited/Ltd. |
| **INFORMATION** (phone) | directory enquiries |
| **INNERSPRING** | interior sprung |
| **INSTALLMENT PLAN** | hire purchase |
| **INTERMISSION** | interval |
| **INTERN** | medical graduate |
| **INTERSECTION** | road junction |

# J

| | |
|---|---|
| **JACKHAMMER** | pneumatic hammer |
| **JACKRABBIT** | hare |
| **JAMMIES** | pyjamas |
| **JAW BREAKER** | gob stopper |
| **JAVA** | coffee |
| **JELLO** | jelly |
| **JELLY ROLL** | Swiss roll |
| **JIBE** (nautical) | tack |
| **JIBE** | agree with, fit in with |
| **JIGGER** | tot |
| **JIMMY** | jemmy |
| **JITNEY** | small bus, jeep |

| U.S.A. | U.K. |
|---|---|
| JIVE | tease, fool; meaningless talk |
| JOCK | athletic male |
| JOHN | toilet |
| JOHN DOE | Joe Bloggs |
| JOHN HENRY/HANCOCK | person's signature |
| JOHNNY-JUMP-UP | violet/pansy |
| JUMBLE | small circular sweet-cake |
| JUMP ROPE | skip rope |

# K

| U.S.A. | U.K. |
|---|---|
| KAFFEE KLATSCH | coffee morning/informal gathering |
| KEDS | plimsolls |
| KEGLER | bowler, skittle player |
| KEISTER | arse |
| KEROSINE/KEROSENE | paraffin |
| KLUTZ | awkward, clumsy |
| KNICKERS | plus fours |
| KNOCK UP | make pregnant |
| KOOK | crazy or eccentric person |
| KUDOS | good show, well done |

# L

| U.S.A. | U.K. |
|---|---|
| LACY | frilly |

| U.S.A. | U.K. |
|---|---|
| **LADYBUG** | ladybird |
| **LADYFINGER** | finger-shaped sponge cake |
| **LAID OFF** | made redundant |
| **LALLYGAG** | to loiter |
| **LAP ROBE** | travelling rug |
| **LAWN BOWLING** | green bowling |
| **LEASE** | let |
| **LEASH** | lead |
| **LEERY** | wary |
| **LEGAL HOLIDAY** | bank holiday |
| **LICENSE PLATE** | vehicle number plate |
| **LIGHTNING BUG** | firefly |
| **LIMA BEAN** | broad bean |
| **LIMP WRIST** | nancy boy |
| **LINE** (stand in) | queue (up) |
| **LINE UP** | identification parade |
| **LIP SYNCH** | mime to recorded music |
| **LIQUOR** | spirits |
| **LIQUOR STORE** | off licence |
| **LIVERWURST** | liver sausage |
| **LOADED FOR BEAR** | fully prepared |
| **LOAN SHARK** | one who charges interest at an unlawful rate |
| **LOBBY** | foyer |
| **LOCATE** | settle at home/business |
| **LOCATOR** | one who determines land boundaries when disputed |

| U.S.A. | U.K. |
|---|---|
| **LOCOMOTIVE ENGINEER** | train driver |
| **LOGE** | front dress circle |
| **LOGGER** | lumberjack |
| **LOGY** | sluggish, lethargic |
| **LONG DOZEN** | baker's dozen (13) |
| **LONG GREEN** | paper money |
| **LOVE SEAT** | settee, usually a two-seater |
| **LUMBER** | unwanted household goods |
| **LUMBER ROOM** | box room |
| **LUMMOX** | clumsy person |
| **LUSH** | an alcoholic |

# M

| U.S.A. | U.K. |
|---|---|
| **MACKINAW** | a warm, belted cloth coat |
| **MAKING OUT** | snogging |
| **MAIL** | post |
| **MAIL CARRIER/MAILMAN** | postal carrier/postman |
| **MAIL DROP** | pillar box |
| **MAIN STEM** | main street |
| **MAJOR LEAGUE** | principal league in professional baseball |
| **MALL (SHOPPING)** | precinct/arcade |
| **MASON JAR** | Killner jar |
| **MEAT GRINDER** | mincer |

| U.S.A. | U.K. |
|---|---|
| **MEDIAN** | central reservation |
| **MEDICAID** | government sponsored medical aid for the needy |
| **MEDICARE** | government insurance program providing medical care for the elderly |
| **MELD** | to blend, combine, mix |
| **MESA** | a high, steep-sided, rocky Plateau |
| **MEZZANINE** | dress circle |
| **MICHIGAN** (card game) | Newmarket |
| **MINOR LEAGUE** | other than the principal (major) league in baseball |
| **MOLASSES** | black treacle |
| **MONEY ORDER** | postal order |
| **MONKEY WRENCH** | adjustable spanner |
| **MOONSHINE** | illicit liquor |
| **MORTICIAN** | undertaker |
| **MOTHER'S DAY** | second Sunday in May |
| **MOTOCROSS** | scrambles |
| **MOVIES** | pictures, films |
| **MOXIE** | courage, daring, energy |
| **MUFFIN** | bun |
| **MUFFLER** (auto) | silencer |
| **MUGWUMP** | one who "sits on the fence" |
| **MULLIGAN** | a meat and vegetable stew |
| **MUTUAL FUND** | unit trust |

# N

| | |
|---|---|
| **NATATORIUM** | indoor swimming pool |
| **NEWSDEALER/NEWSTAND** | newsagent |
| **NEWSHAWK/NEWSHOUND** | reporter |
| **NICKELODEON** | early jukebox |
| **NIGHTSTICK** | truncheon |
| **NIGHT TABLE** | bedside table |
| **911** | 999 |
| **NIPPLE** (on baby bottle) | teat |
| **NONPAREIL** | hundreds and thousands |
| **NOTARIZE** | attest as a notary |
| **NOT HAY** | a lot of money |
| **NOTIONS STORE** | haberdashery |
| **NUKE IT** | cook in a microwave oven |

# O

| | |
|---|---|
| **OFF-COLOR** | somewhat indecent |
| **OFFICE** (doctor's) | surgery |
| **OFF THE RACK** | off the peg |
| **OFF THE WALL** | bizarre, strange |
| **OIL PAN** | sump |
| **ONE WAY TICKET** | single ticket |
| **ON TAP** (beer) | draught |
| **ON THE LAM** | running away |

| U.S.A. | U.K. |
|---|---|
| ON THE NOSE | precisely |
| ORCHESTRA SEATS | stalls |
| ORNERY | unpleasant, cantankerous |
| OUTLET | power point |
| OUTLET PLUG | mains lead |
| OUT OF WHACK | out of order |
| OUT TO LUNCH | crazy |
| OVERPASS | fly over |

# P

| | |
|---|---|
| PACIFIER | dummy |
| PACKAGE | parcel |
| PACKAGE STORE | off license |
| PADDLE (ping pong) | bat (table tennis) |
| PALOOKA | lout, poor performer at sport |
| PANHANDLE | to beg in the street |
| PANHANDLE | narrow projecting strip of land such as in Texas |
| PANTIHOSE | tights |
| PANTYWAIST | nancy boy, effeminate man |
| PANTIES IN A WAD | knickers in a twist |
| PAP SMEAR | cervical smear |
| PARKING LOT | car park |
| PARTICLE BOARD | chipboard |

| U.S.A. | U.K. |
|---|---|
| PASS (vehicle) | overtake |
| PASTOR | vicar |
| PATSY | scapegoat, victimised or deceived person |
| PAVEMENT | roadway |
| PEEPER | private detective |
| PENITENTIARY | prison |
| PEPPER SHAKER | pepper pot |
| PHI BETA KAPPA | member of the oldest college fraternity |
| PICKY | fussy, finicky |
| PINCH HITTER | substitute |
| PINKSTER | Whitsuntide |
| PINOCHLE | pronounced "P nuckle" - card game with double pack (9s to aces only) |
| PINOLE | flour made from parched corn flour |
| PINTO | piebald horse |
| PISSED | angry |
| PIT | stone of a fruit |
| PITCHER | jug |
| PITMAN (mechanism) | connecting rod |
| PLACE BET | horse to be first or second |
| PLUGGED NICKEL | brass farthing |
| PLUG UGLY | ruffian, gangster |
| PODIATRIST | chiropodist |

81

| U.S.A. | U.K. |
|---|---|
| **POLICE CAPTAIN** | police inspector |
| **POLLIWOG** | tadpole |
| **PONDEROSA** | pine tree |
| **PONY CAR** | sporty two-door car |
| **POPSICLE** | iced lolly |
| **POSTAGE METER** | franking machine |
| **POT CHEESE** | cottage cheese |
| **POT HOLDERS/GLOVES** | oven cloth/gloves |
| **POWDERED SUGAR** | icing sugar |
| **PRAIRIE SCHOONER** | large covered wagon |
| **PRECINCT** | district |
| **PREVIEW** (movies) | trailer |
| **PRINCIPAL** | headmaster/mistress |
| **PRIVATE SCHOOL** | public school |
| **PROCTOR** | invigilator |
| **PROM** | school dance |
| **PUBLIC SCHOOL** | school managed by public authorities |
| **PUMP** | ladies court shoe |
| **PURSE** | handbag |
| **PUSSY-WHIPPED** | hen-pecked |
| **PX (post exchange)** | NAAFI |

# Q

| | |
|---|---|
| **QUAHOG** | edible clam |

| U.S.A. | U.K. |
|---|---|
| **QUARTER DAYS** | Jan. 1, Apr. 1, Jul. 1, Oct. 1 |
| **QUARTER HORSE** | horse bred to run strongly over the quarter mile |
| **QUARTER NOTE** | crotchet |
| **QUIRT** | riding crop |
| **QUONSET HUT** | Nissen hut |
| **QUOTATION MARKS** | inverted commas |

# R

| | |
|---|---|
| **RAILROAD TIES** | railway sleepers |
| **RAIN CHECK** | postponement |
| **RAMP** | slip road |
| **RANGE** | cooker |
| **RANGER** | park/forest warden |
| **RATTLER** | goods train; rattlesnake |
| **RAZZ** | tease, deride |
| **REALTOR** | estate agent |
| **REALTY** | real estate |
| **RECAP** (tire) | retread |
| **RECEIPT** | chit |
| **RECESS** (school) | break |
| **RESTROOM** | toilet/W.C. |
| **RESUME** | C.V. (Curriculum Vitae) |
| **RHINESTONE** | diamante |
| **RHUBARB** | expression for a heated dispute |

| U.S.A. | U.K. |
|---|---|
| RIFFED | sacked, made redundant |
| RINKY DINK | old fashioned, dilapidated |
| ROACH | cockroach |
| ROMAINE LETTUCE | cos lettuce |
| ROOKIE | new team member |
| ROOSTER | cockerel |
| ROOT BEER | soda pop made from plant root extracts |
| ROUGH RIDER | person who breaks in horses |
| ROUND TRIP | return |
| ROUSTABOUT | unskilled labourer |
| ROWEN | aftermath, field of stubble |
| ROW HOUSE | terraced house |
| RUBBING ALCOHOL | surgical spirit |
| RUBE | yokel |
| RUBE GOLDBERG | Heath Robinson |
| RUMBLE | fight |
| RUMBLE SEAT | dickey seat |
| RUMPUS ROOM | games room |
| RUTABAGA | swede |

# S

| | |
|---|---|
| SAD SACK | very inept person |
| SALAD DRESSING | salad cream |

| U.S.A. | U.K. |
|---|---|
| **SALES CLERK** | shop assistant |
| **SALUTATORIAN** | second ranking member of a graduating class who delivers an opening speech at graduation |
| **SAND DOLLAR** | round flat sea urchin |
| **SASHAY** | walk ostentatiously/casually |
| **SCADS** | large quantities, lashings |
| **SCALPER** | ticket tout |
| **SCAM** | rip off |
| **SCHEDULE** | timetable |
| **SCHLEMIEL** | foolish or unlucky person |
| **SCHLOCH** | poor quality; secondhand |
| **SCOPE OUT** | check into, investigate |
| **SCOTCH TAPE** | Sellotape |
| **SCRAPPLE** | stewed meat and flour pressed into cakes |
| **SCRATCH PAD** | scribbling pad |
| **SCREEN** | window/door netting, allowing air through, but not insects |
| **SCREWBALL** | strange or crazy person |
| **SCROD** | last/freshest catch of the day |
| **SECOND FLOOR** | first floor |
| **SECOND GUESS** | know by hindsight |
| **SECOND STOREY MAN** | cat burglar |
| **SEDAN** | family car, saloon car |

| U.S.A. | U.K. |
|---|---|
| **SEMESTER** (school) | term |
| **SEND UP** | put in prison |
| **SHAKE DOWN** | extort money from; a raid |
| **SHARK** | outstanding student |
| **SHAVE TAIL** | mule just broken in |
| **SHEDDING** | moulting |
| **SHEERS** | net curtains |
| **SHILL** | person used as a decoy |
| **SHIPPING** | postage |
| **SHIRT WAIST** | blouse |
| **SHOAT** | piglet |
| **SHOO FLY** | temporary road or railway; guard detailed to watch people |
| **SHOO FLY PIE** | sweet treacle dessert |
| **SHOO IN** | a certainty |
| **SHOTS** | jabs, inoculations |
| **SHOWER** | party to give presents to a prospective bride/expectant mother |
| **SHREDDED** (coconut) | desiccated |
| **SHUCK** | remove shells from oysters |
| **SIDEBURNS** | sideboards |
| **SIDEWALK** | pavement |
| **SIDING** | building's exterior cladding |
| **SIGNAL TOWER** | signal box |
| **SILVERWARE** | cutlery |

| U.S.A. | U.K. |
|---|---|
| **SKID ROW** | part of town frequented by vagrants, alcoholics, etc. |
| **SKIN GAME** | swindling game, confidence trick |
| **SKIVVIES** | underwear |
| **SLATE** | schedule; nominate |
| **SLEW** | a large number, many |
| **SLICKER** | a plausible rogue |
| **SLINGSHOT** | catapult |
| **SLIP COVER** | loose cover |
| **SMART-ALEC** | clever dick |
| **SNAP** | easy task |
| **SNAPS** | press studs |
| **SNEAKERS** | plimsolls, gym shoes |
| **SNICKER** | snigger |
| **SNOLLYGOSTER** | shrewd, unscrupulous person |
| **SNOW JOB** | attempt to persuade by misleading talk |
| **SNOWED UNDER** | overwhelmed |
| **SOCKDOLOGER** | decisive blow |
| **SOD** | turf |
| **SODA** | pop, soda pop |
| **SODA CRACKER** | cream cracker |
| **SOLITAIRE** (cards) | patience |
| **SOPHOMORE** | second year student at high school or at a college or university |

| U.S.A. | U.K. |
|---|---|
| SPATULA | fish slice |
| SPIEL | glib or persuasive speech |
| SQUASH | marrow |
| STAKE OUT | to place under surveillance |
| STANDPATTER | opposed to change |
| STAND THE GAFF | endure hardship |
| STATION WAGON | estate car |
| STAY AT HOME | stop at home |
| STEAL (A) | a bargain; easy task |
| STICK SHIFT | manual (gears) |
| STOGY | long cigar |
| STOLE MY THUNDER | said or did something before I could |
| STOOL PIGEON | copper's nark |
| STREETCAR | tram |
| STREET SIGN | signpost |
| STRING BEAN | runner bean |
| STROLLER | push chair |
| STUDIO APT. | a bedsit |
| STYROFOAM | polystyrene |
| SUBDIVISION | housing estate |
| SUBWAY | tube, underground |
| SUCKER | toffy lolly |
| SURF & TURF | a beef and seafood meal |
| SUSPENDERS | braces |
| SWAN DIVE | swallow dive |
| SWEATSUIT | tracksuit |

| U.S.A. | U.K. |
|---|---|
| **SWING SHIFT** | night shift |
| **SWITCHBACK** | road with alternating left and right bends |
| **SWITCHBLADE** | flick knife |

# T

| U.S.A. | U.K. |
|---|---|
| **TAD** | small amount, small boy |
| **TAFFY** | a kind of toffee |
| **TAG** | motor vehicle license plate |
| **TAG DAY** | flag day |
| **TALK TURKEY** | be straightforward |
| **TAR HEEL** | native of North Carolina |
| **TEAMSTER** | lorry driver |
| **TEETER-TOTTER** | seesaw |
| **TEMBLOR** | earthquake |
| **TEXAS GATE** | cattle grid |
| **THUMB TACK** | drawing pin |
| **TICK-TACK-TOE** | noughts and crosses |
| **TIGHTWAD** | miserly person |
| **TILT A WHIRL** | waltzer |
| **TIRE** | tyre |
| **TOTAL** (vehicle) | write off |
| **TOUCH BASE** | contact, get in touch with |
| **TRACTOR TRAILER** | articulated lorry |
| **TRAFFIC CIRCLE** | roundabout |

| U.S.A. | U.K. |
|---|---|
| **TRAILER** | caravan |
| **TRAILER PARK** | caravan site |
| **TRASH CAN** | dustbin |
| **TRICKY** | dodgy |
| **TRUCK FARM** | market garden |
| **TRUCK STOP** | transport cafe |
| **TRUNK** (car) | boot |
| **TUCKERED OUT** | tired out, knackered |
| **TURRET LATHE** | capstan lathe |
| **TURTLENECK** | polo neck |
| **TUXEDO/TUX** | dinner jacket |
| **TWO BIT** | petty, small time |
| **TWO BITS** | 25 cents |

# U

| | |
|---|---|
| **UNDERGRADUATES** | |
|   **FRESHMAN** | 1st year |
|   **SOPHOMORE** | 2nd year |
|   **JUNIOR** | 3rd year |
|   **SENIOR** | 4th year |
| **UNLISTED NUMBER** | ex-directory |
| **UP CHUCK** | vomit |
| **U.S. POSTAL SERVICE** | Royal Mail |
| **UTILITY LINES** | mains |

| U.S.A. | U.K. |
|---|---|

# V

| | |
|---|---|
| **VALANCE** | pelmet |
| **VALEDICTORIAN** | highest ranking student in a graduating class who gives graduation farewell speech |
| **VEST** | waistcoat |
| **VETERAN** | ex-serviceman |
| **VETERANS' DAY** | Remembrance Day |
| **VOUCHER** | chit |

# W

| | |
|---|---|
| **WALKING PAPERS** | marching orders, dismissal |
| **WALL-TO-WALL CARPET** | fitted carpet |
| **WASH CLOTH** | face flannel |
| **WASH UP** | wash hands and face |
| **WAVE** (Women's navy) | WREN |
| **WAXED PAPER** | greaseproof paper |
| **WAY STATION** | minor railway station, a halt |
| **WET BACK** | illegal immigrant from Mexico |
| **WHAMMY** | hex, setback, shocking blow |
| **WHISTLE-STOP** | minor railway station, a halt |
| **WHOLE NOTE** | semibreve |

| U.S.A. | U.K. |
|---|---|
| **WICKET** | small sliding window or opening (e.g. at a ticket office) |
| **WIND BREAKER** | wind cheater |
| **WINDSHIELD** | windscreen |
| **WINGDING** | wild party |
| **WITH OR WITHOUT** (milk) | white or black |
| **WRECKER** | breakdown lorry |
| **WRIST PIN** | gudgeon pin |

# Y

| | |
|---|---|
| **YARD** | garden of a house |
| **YARD SALE** | house clearance sale |
| **YAWP** | to cry out; to talk continually and noisily |
| **YEGG** | burglar, safecracker |
| **YELLOW DOG** | mongrel; someone anti-union |
| **Y'ALL (YOU ALL)** | you |
| **YUP** | yes |

# Z

| | |
|---|---|
| **Z** | Zed |

| U.S.A. | U.K. |
|---|---|
| **ZILCH** | nothing |
| **ZINGER** | sharp witticism |
| **ZIP** | nil, no score |
| **ZIP CODE** | postal code |
| **ZIT** | spot |
| **ZUCCHINI** | courgette |

# RHYMING SLANG

Rhyming slang is a type of code said to have been invented by the Cockneys who resented having to work with Irish immigrants. They devised the rhyming words to not be understood. Here are some examples:

| | |
|---|---|
| Adam and Eve | I believe |
| Alligator | Later |
| Andy Cain | Rain |
| Apples and pears | Stairs |
| Bacon and eggs | Legs |
| Bat and wicket | Ticket |
| Bees and honey | Money |
| Bell ringers | Fingers |
| Bin Lids | Kids |
| Biscuits and cheese | Knees |
| Bride and groom | Broom |
| Brown hat | Cat |
| Bug and flea | Tea |
| Butcher's hook | Look |
| Carving knife | Wife |
| Cat and mouse | House |
| Corns and bunions | Onions |
| Cough and sneeze | Cheese |
| Cow and calf | Laugh |
| Currant bun | Son |
| Dickory dock | Clock |
| Dickey dirt | Shirt |
| Dot and carried | Married |
| Flounder and dab | Taxicab |
| Frog and Toad | Road |

| | |
|---|---|
| Gay and frisky | Whisky |
| German flutes | Boots |
| Glorious sinner | Dinner |
| Ham shank | Yank |
| Hit or miss | Kiss |
| Jack and Jill | Till, Bill |
| Jumbo's trunk | Drunk |
| Khyber Pass | Glass |
| Kidney punch | Lunch |
| Lean and lurch | Church |
| Lion's lair | Chair |
| London Fog | Dog |
| Lucky locket | Pocket |
| Mince pies | Eyes |
| Needle and thread | Bread |
| Peas in the pot | Hot |
| Pen and ink | Drink/Stink |
| Pig's ear | Beer |
| Pimple and wart | Quart |
| Potatoes in the mould | Cold |
| Pull down the shutter | Butter |
| Read and write | Fight |
| Rub-a-dub club | Pub |
| Skin and blister | Sister |
| Struggle and strain | Train |
| Ted Frazor | Razor |
| Tommy Tucker | Supper |
| Turtle doves | Gloves |
| Whistle and Flute | Suit |
| Uncle Ned | Bed |
| Zinc pail | British Rail |

## PRONUNCIATION GUIDE

In addition to different spellings, words may be pronounced differently in the U.K. and U.S. A., such as these:

|  | American | British |
|---|---|---|
| Aluminum* | alumin NUMB | AL-lu-MIN-e-um |
| Albino | al-bye-no | al-bean-o |
| Anti | an tie | ant ee |
| Azores | a-zores | uhzores |
| Arctic | ardic | arc tic |
| Banana | buh nan na | buh nah na |
| Buoy | boo-eee | boy |
| Caramel | car mul | cara mell |
| Charades | sha raids | sha rahds |
| Chassis | chassee | shassee |
| Clerk | klerk | klark |
| Controversy | CON tro ver see | con TRO ver see |
| Era | erra | ear ra |
| Data | dadda | day ta |
| Half | haff | hahf |
| Herbs | erbs | herbs |
| Iodine | eye o dine | eye o dean |
| Laboratory | LAB ra tory | la BOR a tory |
| Leisure | lee shur | lehzure |
| Privacy | pry va see | priv uh see |
| Quasi | kwaz eye | kwazee |
| Schedule | sked yule | shed yule |
| Status | stadous | stay tus |
| Tomato | to may toe | to maa toe |

*spelled *aluminium* in U.K.

# TEMPERATURE CONVERSIONS

Degress F (Farenheit ) to Degrees C (Celsius/Centigrade)

Take Farenheit temperature, subtract 32 degrees and multiply
by 5/9; or take the Celsius temperature, multiply by 9/5 and
add 32 degrees.

| FARENHEIT (F) | CELSIUS (C) |
|:---:|:---:|
| 104 | 40 |
| 98.6 | 37 |
| 95 | 35 |
| 86 | 30 |
| 77 | 25 |
| 68 | 20 |
| 59 | 15 |
| 41 | 5 |
| 32 | 0 |
| 23 | -5 |
| 14 | -10 |
| 5 | -15 |
| 0 | -18 |
| -9 | -23 |
| -18 | -28 |
| -40 | -40 |

# COMPARATIVE SIZES AND MEASURES

Imperial Pint            approx. 20 fluid ounces
U.S. pint                = 16 fluid ounces
Imperial Gallon         approx. 157 fluid ounces
U.S. gallon             = 128 fluid ounces
U.K. hundred weight    = 112 pounds
U.S. hundred weight     = 100 pounds

To further complicate the issue, the U.K. fluid ounce varies slightly from the U.S. fluid ounce.

The U.S. gallon = approx. 4/5 of the U.K. gallon, or the U.K. gallon is 1 ¼ times the U.S. gallon.

NOTE: In U.K. a person's weight is measured in "stones." A stone is equal to 14 pounds.

## U.K. TO U.S.A. COMPARATIVE SIZES

Since clothing and shoe manufacturers vary, the comparisons made here are approximate. Generally, U.K. shoe sizes are 1 to 1½ sizes lower than the U.S. sizes. For example, a men's size 9 in the U.K. is about a 10 in the U.S.; a woman's size 6 U.K. is about a 7½ in the U.S. Women's dresses may run 2 sizes lower in the U.S. (14 U.K. is 12 U.S.). Metric sizes are also used.

**ELECTRICITY**    U.K. 220 volts, A.C. 50 cycles
                      U.S.   120 volts, 60 cycles

**EMERGENCIES:**    U.K. dial 999         U.S. dial 911